Catholic Faith Teaching Manual

Level 5 : Confirmation

Copyright © 2021 by Father Raymond Taouk. All rights reserved.

"No part of this publication may be reproduced, distributed, or transmitted in any form or by any means, including photocopying, recording, or other electronic or mechanical methods, or by any information storage and retrieval system without the prior written permission of the publisher, except in the case of very brief quotations embodied in critical reviews and certain other noncommercial uses permitted by copyright law."

Co published with JMJ Catholic products.
www.jmjcatholicproducts.com.au
Email : jeanette@jmjcatholicproducts.com.au

ISBN: 9780645021936

TABLE OF CONTENTS

		Page
Lesson 1	Catechism : The doctrine of the Trinity (Questions 14, 15, 16, 16a, 16b)	6
	Prayer : Apostles Creed	7
	Bible Studies : The election of Mattias and decent of the holy spirit.	8
	The Saints : Saint Ambrose	11
	Confirmation : The Ten Commandments	15
	Church History : The first years of Christianity (from 32 Ad to 70 AD)	16
Lesson 2	Catechism : The doctrine of the incarnation (Questions 40, 41, 42, 43)	20
	Prayer : Apostles Creed (cont'd)	21
	Bible Studies : A Lane man cured by Peter and John	22
	Bible Studies : Ananias and Saphira	23
	The Saints : Saint Patrick	25
	Confirmation : The Precepts of the Church	27
	Church History : The first years of Christianity (The First Century)	28
Lesson 3	Catechism : The doctrine of the incarnation (Questions 44, 45, 45a, 45b)	32
	Prayer : Apostles Creed (cont'd)	33
	Bible Studies : The Twelve Apostles in Prison, Gamaliel's Council	34
	The Saints : Saint Columba	37
	Confirmation : The Divine Institution of Confirmation	39
	Church History : The first Century	40
Lesson 4	Catechism : The doctrine of the incarnation (Questions 45c, 45d, 45e)	44
	Prayer : Apostles Creed (cont'd)	45
	Bible Studies : The election of Deacons - Stephen the first Martyr	46
	The Saints : Saint Gregory VII	49
	Confirmation : Nature of Confirmation	51
	Church History : Persecutions	53
Lesson 5	Catechism : The Doctrine of Redemption (Questions 46, 47, 48, 49)	56
	Prayer : Apostles Creed (cont'd)	57
	Bible Studies : Baptism of the officer of Queen Candace	58
	The Saints : Saint Norbert	61
	Confirmation : The minister of Confirmation	63
	Church History : Heresies, The enemy within	64
Lesson 6	Catechism : The Doctrine of Redemption (Questions 50, 51, 52)	68
	Prayer : The Act of Faith	69
	Bible Studies : The conversion of Saul	70
	The Saints : Saint Francis of Assisi	73
	Confirmation : Dispositions for confirmation	75
	Church History : Fathers of the Church	76
Lesson 7	Catechism : The Sacraments (Questions 138, 139, 140)	80
	Prayer : The Act of Hope	81
	Bible Studies : Peter's Journey - He raises Tabitha to life	82
	The Saints : Saint Albert the Great	84
	Confirmation : The ceremonies of Confirmation	86
	Church History : Monks, monasteries and monasticism	88

Lesson 8	Catechism : The Sacraments (Questions 141, 142, 143)		92
	Prayer : The Act of Charity		93
	Bible Studies : The conversion of Cornelius		94
	The Saints : Saint Catherine of Siena		95
	Confirmation : Sponsors and Parents		98
	Church History : Monks, monasteries and monasticism (cont'd)		100
Lesson 9	Catechism : The Sacraments (Questions 144, 145, 146)		104
	Prayer : The Act of Contrition		105
	Bible Studies : Peter in Prison		106
	The Saints : Saint John Of God		109
	Confirmation : The seven gifts of the Holy Ghost		111
	Church History : The temporal power of the Popes		112
Lesson 10	Catechism : Baptism (Questions 147, 148, 149, 150)		116
	Prayer : The Act of Contrition		117
	Bible Studies : Saint Paul's first mission (AD 45 to 48)		118
	The Saints : Saint Camillus De Lellis		120
	Confirmation : The seven gifts of the Holy Ghost (cont'd)		122
	Church History : Mohammedanism		123
Lesson 11	Catechism : Confirmation (Questions 151, 152, 153)		126
	Prayer : The Confiteor		127
	Bible Studies : The Council of Jerusalem (AD 51)		128
	The Saints : Saint Vincent De Paul		131
	Confirmation : The 12 fruits of the Holy Ghost		133
	Church History : The Great schism in the East		134
Lesson 12	Catechism : The Holy Eucharist (Questions 154, 155, 156)		138
	Prayer : The Confiteor (cont'd)		139
	Bible Studies : The second mission of Saint Paul (AD 51 to 54)		141
	The Saints : Saint Alphonsus Liguori		143
	Confirmation : Christian Perfection		146
	Church History : The Crusades		148
Lesson 13	Catechism : The Holy Eucharist (Questions 157, 158, 159)		152
	Prayer : Prayer to the Holy Ghost		153
	Bible Studies : Saint Paul's third mission (AD 55 to 58)		154
	The Saints : Saint Therese of Lisieux		154
	Confirmation : General means of perfection		158
	Church History : Popes of the ninth century to the thirteenth century		159
Lesson 14	Catechism : The Holy Sacrifice of the Mass (Questions 160, 161, 162)		164
	Prayer : Prayer to the Holy Ghost		165
	Bible Studies : Last years of the life of the Apostles		166
	The Saints : Saint Elizabeth of Hungary		168
	Confirmation : General means of perfection - self denial		170
	Church History : The Avignon Popes - The Western Schism		171
Lesson 15	Catechism Questions		176

Lesson 1

Level 5

Confirmation

Catechism

You will continue in this level to study your catechism questions. They are to be learned by heart as they are the very backbone of your studies. Level 4 finished at question number 136. You will notice over the first six lessons, that we have changed the number order, having repeated some questions from previous lessons and having added some questions from other areas; this is because this level is specifically for the preparation of the Sacrament of Confirmation and the questions included are minimal required knowledge for the receiving of the Sacrament. This actually makes no difference to your studying of the questions, just to the numbers next to the questions themselves.

The Doctrine of the Trinity

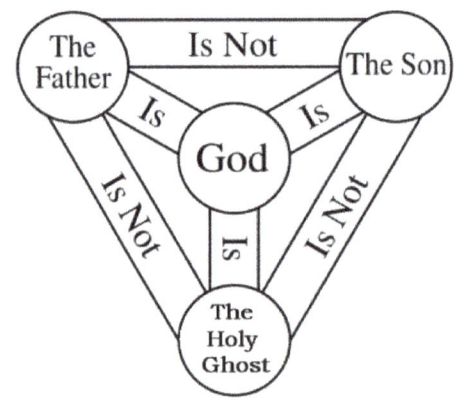

14. **Is there only one God?**

    Yes, there is only one God.

15. **How many Persons are there in God?**

    *In God there are three Divine Persons
    - the Father, the Son, and the Holy Ghost.*

16. **What do we mean by the Blessed Trinity?**

    By the Blessed Trinity we mean one and the same God in three Divine Persons.

16a **How are the three Divine Persons, though really distinct from one another, one and the same God?**

The three Divine Persons, though really distinct from one another, are one and the same God, because all have one and the same Divine Nature.

16b **Can we fully understand how the three Divine Persons, though really distinct from one another, are one and the same God?**

We cannot fully understand how the three Divine Persons, though really distinct from one another, are one and the same God, because this is a supernatural mystery.

The mystery of the Blessed Trinity is one of the most important doctrines of the Church. The fact that God is one, but at the same time, is three Persons, is beyond our nature to comprehend. We believe this because God has revealed it to us. When some young people don't understand something, they say 'it is stupid'. But no, it is not 'it' that is stupid. It is our lack of knowledge and understanding. The mystery of the Blessed Trinity is at the heart of our faith.

Prayer

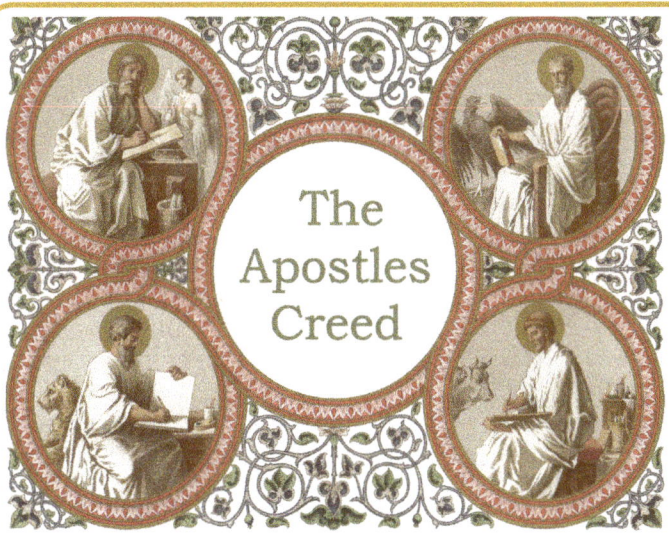

In this level, as in Level Four, we are going to study the meanings of the words in the prayers we pray. The Apostles' Creed is a prayer that outlines the chief truths of our faith. We start our Rosary with this prayer and it is important that we understand the meaning of these words.

The word Creed comes from Latin, Credo, which means I believe. Therefore, the Creed is a summary of what one believes. It is called the The Apostles' Creed because it was composed by the Apostles, and contains a summary of the principal truths they taught.

The Apostles' Creed has come down to us intact, except for a few clauses added by the Church later, in order to counteract various heresies. These additions, however, are not new doctrines, but a clarification of what the Creed already contained.

The Creed is divided into twelve articles and all the articles are absolutely necessary to faith; if even one article is omitted or changed, faith would be destroyed.

I believe in God, the Father Almighty, Creator of heaven and earth;

This first article teaches us that God is the creator of all things on earth and in heaven. It also shows us the First Person of the Blessed Trinity, to Whom creation is attributed. This is the beginning of the teaching of the Holy Trinity.

And in Jesus Christ, His only Son, Our Lord;

This second article of the Creed shows our faith in the Second Person of the Blessed Trinity and His relation to God the Father, that is, the Son.

Question 1 ❖ How many Persons are there in God?
Question 2 ❖ How are the three Divine Persons, though really distinct from one another, one and the same God?
Question 3 ❖ What do we mean by the Blessed Trinity?
Question 4 ❖ What does the word Credo mean?
Question 5 ❖ How many articles of faith does the Apostles' Creed contain?
Question 6 ❖ What does the first article of the Apostles' Creed teach us?

Bible Studies

In this Level we will be looking at stories from the Acts of the Apostles, written by Saint Luke. This was the beginning of the spread of Christianity. The Apostles were confirmed on the first Pentecost Sunday, when the Holy Ghost appeared to them under the form of tongues of fire. From there, they went out and spread the gospel at the risk of their own lives.

The Election of Matthias and the Descent of the Holy Ghost

Descending from Mount Olivet, the apostles retired to the upper chamber, or supper-room of the house in which they usually assembled. There they remained in prayer for ten days, with Mary the mother of Jesus, several other holy women, and a great number of disciples, the number of persons being about one hundred and twenty. During those days of prayer, Peter, rising up, said that it was time for a new apostle to be chosen to replace the traitor Judas.

The choice had come down to two men, Joseph, called Barsabbas, and Matthias. After praying for guidance, the Apostle cast their vote, and they chose Matthias, who was numbered with the eleven apostles, and filled the place left vacant by the lamentable fall of Judas. Ten days after the ascension, the Jews celebrated the Feast of Pentecost.

On that day the apostles were assembled together, persevering in prayer, when suddenly there came a sound from heaven as of a mighty rushing of wind, and it filled the whole house where they were sitting. There appeared to them cloven tongues, as it were of fire, and it sat upon every one of them. And they were filled with the Holy Ghost, and began to speak in divers tongues (different languages).

Now, there were at that time, in Jerusalem, Jews from every nation under heaven, who had come for the celebration of the feast. Having heard of what had taken place, they went in great numbers to the house wherein the apostles were assembled. Each one was astonished to hear them speak in his own tongue (language).

But some of the people mocked them, saying that they were drunk. Then Peter, going forth from the house with the other apostles, lifted up his voice, and spoke, "These are not drunk, as you suppose, but this is that which was spoken of by the prophet Joel: 'In the last days I will pour out of My Spirit upon all flesh, and your sons and your daughters shall prophesy.' "Ye men of Israel, hear these words: Jesus of Nazareth, a man approved of God among you by miracles, and wonders, and signs, which God did by Him in the midst of you, as you also know; Him you have crucified and put to death by the hands of wicked men. God hath raised Him up, whereof we all are witnesses. Being exalted, therefore, by the right hand of God, and having received of the Father the promise of the Holy Ghost, He hath poured forth this which you see and hear. Therefore, let all the house of Israel know most assuredly that God hath made Him Lord and Christ, this same Jesus whom you have crucified."

Level 5 - Lesson 1

Bible Studies

The words of Peter had a divine power that penetrated all hearts, and many, repenting of their sins, asked Peter and the other apostles what they ought to do. Peter said to them: "Do penance, and be baptized, everyone of you, in the name of Jesus Christ for the remission of your sins, and you shall receive the gift of the Holy Ghost."

They received his words with joy, and on that day about three thousand persons were baptized.

Question 7 ❖ Why did the Apostles choose another Apostle?
Question 8 ❖ Who was chosen to take the place of Judas?
Question 9 ❖ On what day did the Holy Ghost come to the Apostles?
Question 10 ❖ How many people were baptized on the first Pentecost?

Level 5 - Lesson 1

The Saints

Saint Ambrose

Ambrose was born in the year 340, not very many years after Emperor Constantine had made Christianity the religion of the Roman Empire. At that time the Empire had four great governors, and one of these, the Prefect of Gaul (who was responsible for Britain, France, Spain, Portugal, as well as parts of Germany, and for the islands of Sardinia, Corsica, and Sicily), was Ambrose's father. It was natural that Ambrose too should train to become a governor, and he was sent to Rome to prepare himself for his career. When he was twenty-nine he was made Governor of Northern Italy and went to live in the great palace at Milan, where at that time was the Court of the Emperor of the West. He ruled well, and the people came to love and trust him.

Five years after Ambrose became governor the Bishop of Milan died, and there was such a dispute as to who should become the next Bishop that on the day of the election Ambrose decided that he, as Governor, ought to attend in state in case the two different parties began to fight. He spoke to the people, reminding them how they should behave on such a solemn day. Then in silence after he had finished speaking a child's voice suddenly called out: "Ambrose, Bishop." It seemed like a sign from Heaven. The crowds took up the cry, and the Governor found himself faced by the whole city roaring, "Ambrose must be our bishop."

But Ambrose was not a priest. It was quite impossible for him, said Ambrose, to become their bishop. He was their governor, and their governor he would remain. Then, when they still called for him as bishop, he decided to run away. He left secretly at night by a side-door of the palace, and started to travel to Rome. But in the dark he took the wrong turn, and just as day broke he found that he had gone in a circle and had come back to Milan again by another gate. This time the people surrounded him in his palace, and he was practically made a prisoner. So at last he gave in, was baptized, and seven days later made Bishop of Milan. He was thirty-four, and for the remaining twenty-three years of his life he stayed in Milan as Bishop.

He had found when he was governor that it had been difficult to raise enough money to keep the city in proper repair; but with his power then he had been able to tax the people. Now that he had to keep the churches in repair and to find money for the poor he found things still more difficult. He gave away to the Church all his own money and possessions, and made others follow his example. And when people were starving and no more money could be found he decided to sell the gold and silver vessels of the Church itself. His enemies said that this was an insult to God.

"Which do you think is more valuable," said Ambrose, "church vessels or living souls?" And he went on selling the treasures in the market-place, calling, "Behold, the God of Christ that saves men from death!"

The Saints

Ambrose's enemies were people called Arians, who claimed to be Christians but who did not really believe that Jesus was God. The Empress herself and most of the courtiers and the wealthy people of Milan were Arians, and at last the Empress, who hated Ambrose, determined to take one of the Christian churches to use for Arian worship. Because she was the head of the State she had the right to take any building she wanted, but, all the same, Ambrose knew he must refuse her. He would not allow a Catholic church to be taken for Arian services. "Palaces are matters for the Emperor," he said, "but churches belong to the Bishop."

The Empress would not listen to his arguments, but ordered her soldiers to occupy one of the churches of Milan. Then Ambrose called on the faithful Christians, and day after day, night after night, they filled every church in the city, saying their prayers, singing hymns, and listening to sermons, so that there was not room for a single soldier to get inside a church. The citizens who had insisted that Ambrose should become Bishop now showed how loyal they were to him. And on Good Friday, 386, the Empress admitted she was beaten and withdrew her order.

Ambrose's next step was to build a great new cathedral (which is known today as Saint Ambrose's) in which he determined to make a shrine for two martyrs, the twin brothers Gervase and Protase, who had given their lives for Christ in Milan over two hundred years before in one of the great persecutions. But no one knew where the martyrs had been buried, and the people did not want to wait until their bones were found – if ever they could be sure that the saints themselves would make it possible for him to discover their tomb; and one night the answer was given to him in a dream.

Next day he ordered the workmen to dig in a certain place in front of the railing of a churchyard outside the city gates. The hole was dug, but there was no sign of any bodies buried there. But when it seemed that he had made a mistake an extraordinary thing happened. Blind and lame and sick people who had gone to the place, hoping to find the relics there, were suddenly cured. So the digging began again, and at last the two bodies were found and taken in state to be reburied in the new cathedral. One of the immense multitude who watched was an African name Augustine, who was later baptized by Ambrose and became one of the greatest of Christian saints.

At the doors of the new cathedral some time later occurred an event which was one of the great landmarks of the early Christian church. In a town far from Milan the Governor had put in prison a charioteer who was a favorite of the people at the games in the Circus. The people thought the sentence was unjust, and they became so angry that they murdered the Governor. When the news of it was brought to the Emperor, who was in Milan, he swore that he would take terrible vengeance on the town. Ambrose came to the Emperor, and, while not making light of the crime, asked him to be merciful. Ambrose thought that the Emperor had listened to him, but actually the Emperor sent secret orders to the soldiers of the town that there was to be a great massacre, and seven thousand men, women, and children were murdered.

Level 5 - Lesson 1

The Saints

When the news came to Milan, Ambrose called the Emperor a murderer and refused to allow him to receive the sacraments until he had done penance in public. The Emperor said he was sorry, and came to the Cathedral in state, accompanied by his courtiers and his guards. But at the door Ambrose barred the way.

"How can you lift up in prayer the hands that are still dripping with blood?" said Ambrose. "Depart, I say."

"David sinned," said the Emperor; "yet David was forgiven."

"Yes," said Ambrose, "you have imitated David in his sin. Now imitate him in his repentance." And not until the Emperor put off all his royal clothes and put on sackcloth and in the sight of all Milan confessed his sin, promised amendment, and lay on his face before the High Altar was he allowed once more to receive Holy Communion.

That he was indeed sorry we know, because he enacted a new law that between the pronouncement of a sentence of death and its execution a whole month must pass, so that there would be time to prevent any injustice. And the Emperor so loved and respected Ambrose for showing that the law of God is greater than the law of even the most powerful man that he said, "Ambrose is the only man I think worthy of the name Bishop."

Question 11 ◆ Saint Ambrose became bishop of where?
Question 12 ◆ Which great Saint was baptized by Saint Ambrose?
Question 13 ◆ How old was Saint Ambrose when he was consecrated a bishop?

Level 5 - Lesson 1

Confirmation

In previous levels, there is a section titled 'Devotions'. In this Level, we are replacing the 'Devotions' section, with a section called, Confirmation. Each lesson does not necessarily teach directly about the Sacrament itself, but it contains the knowledge necessary to prepare for the reception of the Sacraments. Therefore, some of the work presented in this section will be a revision of work from other levels.

The Ten Commandments

A knowledge of the Ten Commandments is essential for all Catholics, especially those who are confirmed and are therefore adult Catholics, soldiers of Christ. These Ten Commandments need to be learned by heart if not already known. The first three commandments are directly related to God and the last seven commandments are directly related to one's neighbor.

1. I am the Lord, thy God; thou shalt not have strange gods before Me.

2. Thou shalt not take the name of the Lord thy God in vain.

3. Remember thou keep holy the Lord's Day.

4. Honor thy father and thy mother.

5. Thou shalt not kill.

6. Thou shalt not commit adultery.

7. Thou shalt not steal.

8. Thou shalt not bear false witness against thy neighbor.

9. Thou shalt not covet thy neighbor's wife.

10. Thou shalt not covet thy neighbor's goods.

Question 14 ❖ How many commandments of God are there?
Question 15 ❖ Which commandments are directly related to God?
Question 16 ❖ Write out and number the seven commandments directly related to our neighbor.

Church History

The First Years of Christianity
From 32AD to 70AD

Our Lord, Jesus Christ, founded a visible Society, or Church to carry on His work through the ages. He handed on His own authority to His twelve Apostles, with Peter appointed as head, about the year 32 AD. Jesus said, "All power is given to Me in Heaven and on Earth. Go ye therefore and teach all nations…. I am with you all days even to the end of the world". So the Church was sent to teach all Nations with the same Divine authority as Jesus Himself. Jesus gave the same mission to His Church as that given to Him. "As the Father sent Me, I also send you." The twelve Apostles were a group of Jews, unlearned, mostly fishermen. The task given to them was quite beyond them unless they were given strength and guidance from God. So it was that Jesus promised to stay with them until the end of time. He also promised to send the Holy Ghost, who would teach them all things.

On Pentecost Sunday, the Holy Ghost came down upon the Apostles and Our Lady in the form of tongues of fire. The Holy Ghost came to strengthen and enlighten the Apostles and to guard and guide the Church through all ages. Pentecost Sunday was the birthday of the Church, because on that day, the Apostles set out to begin their mission of converting the whole world. Saint Peter, by the power of his preaching converted three thousand people with his first sermon.

When Saint Peter and Saint John cured a man crippled from birth and taught that it was done by the power of Jesus, five thousand more people were converted and baptized. The Chief Priests, who had caused the death of Jesus, were very angry to hear the Apostles preaching about Jesus. Saint Peter and Saint John were thrown into jail, scourged and forbidden to preach about Jesus.

Each day, the number of baptized increased. There were many miracles. The Chief Priests were enraged. They started a general persecution of the Church. Saint Stephen was the first put to death by stoning. A man named Saul was there and approved. Saul was one of the great enemies of the Church. Later, on the way to Damascus, Saul was struck down by a light from Heaven and rose up to become the great Saint Paul.

At first the Apostles taught in and around Jerusalem and then they went out to all Judea, Syria, Arabia and Persia. Everywhere there were miracles, more converts, Churches established, bishops and priests ordained. Saint Bartholomew went to Persia, Saint Thomas went to India, Saint Matthew to Ethiopia, Saint Jude to Arabia, Saint Andrew to Greece. All died martyrs for the Faith.

Saint Peter first went to Antioch, the chief Roman city of the East. It was there that the followers of Christ were first called Christians. In 42 AD Saint Peter went to Rome, the capital of the Roman World. After twenty five years in Rome Saint Peter died on a cross (upside down), a martyr for the Faith, in 67 AD.

Question 17 ❖ What was Saint Paul's name before he was converted?
Question 18 ❖ What day is considered to be the birthday of the Church?
Question 19 ❖ Who was the first martyr (person who died for the faith)?

Lesson 2

Level 5

Confirmation

Catechism

The Doctrine of the Incarnation

40. Did God abandon man after Adam fell into sin?

God did not abandon man after Adam fell into sin, but promised to send into the world a Saviour to free man from his sins and to reopen to him the gates of heaven.

41. Who is the Saviour of all men?

The Saviour of all men is Jesus Christ.

42. What is the chief teaching of the Catholic Church about Jesus Christ?

The chief teaching of the Catholic Church about Jesus Christ is that He is God made man.

43. Is Jesus Christ more than one Person?

No, Jesus Christ is only one Person; and that Person is the second Person of the Blessed Trinity.

Question 1   ❖ Did God abandon man after Adam fell into sin?
Question 2   ❖ What is the chief teaching of the Catholic Church about Jesus Christ?
Question 3   ❖ How are the three Divine Persons, though really distinct from one another, one and the same God?

Level 5 - Lesson 2

Prayer

The Apostles' Creed
(*continued*)

Who was conceived by the Holy Ghost, born of the Virgin Mary;

This third article of the Creed affirms the Incarnation; that is, that Christ became man, through the power of the Third Person of the Blessed Trinity, the Holy Ghost. It further testifies that Mary is truly the Mother of Our Lord and God, Jesus Christ.

Suffered under Pontius Pilate, was crucified, died, and was buried.

The fourth article of the Apostles' Creed reminds us of the fact that our Divine Saviour suffered a great agony for our sins to the point of crucifixion upon a Roman Cross in the historical time of Pontius Pilate. It also affirms that He was buried.

He descended into hell; the third day He arose again from the dead.

This fifth article shows that Our Lord was in the tomb for three days. A number of modern heretics, trying to disprove the resurrection, say that Our Lord never died. Well, the Creed states He was dead for three days. After being buried, Jesus descended not to the place of everlasting torment, but to the Limbo of the Fathers; that is, the place where the good and holy people from the Old Testament were waiting until the Gates of Heaven were opened. Jesus brought them the good news that He had died for them and that after His Ascension they would follow Him to heaven.

Question 4 ❖ What does the third article of the Apostles' Creed affirm?
Question 5 ❖ Why is it important to affirm that Jesus really died?
Question 6 ❖ What does the word *Credo* mean?

Bible Studies

A lame Man Cured by Peter and John

They are brought before the Council

One day, Peter and John were going up to the temple to pray. There was at the gate called the Beautiful, a man who was lame from his birth, and who was carried everyday to the gate of the temple to beg alms from those who went in. Seeing Peter and John he asked them for an alms. But Peter said to him: "Silver and gold I have none, but what I have I give thee: In the name of Jesus Christ of Nazareth, rise up and walk!"

Then having taken the man by the right hand, Peter lifted him up, and immediately his feet and soles became firm. Then, leaping up, he stood and walked, and entered with them into the temple, praising and blessing God. All the people were filled with amazement to see the lame man walking and leaping. But Peter said to them: "Ye men of Israel, why wonder you at this? Or why look you upon us as if by our strength we had made this man to walk? The God of our fathers hath glorified His Son Jesus, whom you delivered up to death. The faith which is by Him has given this perfect soundness in the sight of you all. I know that you did it through ignorance. Be penitent, therefore, and be converted, that your sins may be blotted out!"

Many of those who heard these words were converted. But while the apostles were yet speaking to the people, the priests and the officers of the temple came and arrested them, placing them into prison, where they remained until the following day. Then the chief-priests and the ancients had the apostles brought before them, and asked: "By what power, or in whose name have you done this?" Peter answered: "Be it known to you all, and to all the people of Israel, that in the name of our Lord Jesus Christ of Nazareth, whom you crucified, whom God hath raised from the dead, even by Him, doth this man stand here before you whole."

The chief-priests and the ancients ordered Peter and John to be taken out, and said one to another: "What shall we do to these men? For a miracle, indeed, has been done by them, with witnesses of Jerusalem; who saw the miracle, we cannot deny it. But we may no further divulge among the people, let us threaten them, that they speak no more of this miracle to anybody." Then, calling the two apostles, they warned them not to speak at all in the name of Jesus. But they answered them, saying: "If it be just in the sight of God to hear you rather than God, judge me, for we cannot but speak the things which we have seen and heard."

Level 5 - Lesson 2

Bible Studies

Ananias and Saphira

When Peter and John told the disciples all that had taken place, they were excited to great fervor, and prayed that God might strengthen them in the faith, and work signs and wonders by their hands. While they prayed, the place wherein they were, was shaken, and the Holy Ghost coming upon them, imparted to them the gift of courage and the spirit of concord.

They persevered in the doctrine of the apostles, in prayer and in the breaking of the bread; that is, the apostles celebrated the Holy Sacrifice of the Mass, and the faithful received Holy Communion. As such they became so perfect that, of their own accord, they sold all they had, and collected all the money they had made and gave it to the poor.

It so happened that a certain man, named Ananias, with his wife Saphira, sold a piece of land, and brought a portion of the money to the apostles. They acted as if they had given all the money; yet they kept a part for themselves. But Peter said: "Ananias, why has Satan tempted your heart that you should lie to the Holy Ghost, and by fraud keep part of the money for yourself? While it remained, did it not remain to God? And being sold, was it not in Gods power? Why have you conceived this thing in thy heart? You have not lied to men, but to God." Ananias, hearing these words, fell down and died.

Great fear came upon all who heard it, and the young men, rising up, carried away the body. About three hours after, Saphira, the wife of Ananias, came in, and Peter addressed her, saying: "Tell me whether you sold the land for so much?" She answered: "Yes, for so much." Then Peter rebuked her sharply: "Why have you agreed together to tempt the Spirit of the Lord?

"Behold, the feet of those who have buried your husband are at the door, and they shall carry you out!" Immediately she was struck dead at his feet, and the young men, coming in, carried her out also, and buried  her with her husband. This terrible punishment of Ananias and Saphira ought to inspire us with a salutary fear of sinning against the truth.

Question 7 ❖ When Saint Peter made a man walk, who did he attribute it to?
Question 8 ❖ What lesson should we learn from the story of Ananias and Saphira?
Question 9 ❖ How many people were baptized on the first Pentecost?

The Saints

Saint Patrick

One of the companions whom Saint Germain chose to go with him to Britain was a young man named Patrick who, a few years before, had come to him to study for the priesthood at Auxerre. Patrick had arrived there after many adventures. He was the son of a Roman officer stationed in Britain, and had lead the life of an ordinary boy in a wealthy household until, when he was sixteen, he was carried off in a pirate's raid, taken to Ireland and sold as a slave to a chieftain named Milcho. Here his head was shaved, as a sign that he was no longer free; he was given a slave's tunic – a sheepskin reaching down to his knees, and leather sandals – and to be a swineherd on the slopes of Mount Slemish. "I was chastened exceedingly and humbled every day", he later wrote about these years, "in hunger and nakedness."

At last he determined to escape. He walked two hundred miles through unknown country until he reached a port where a ship was sailing for Brittany, and persuaded the captain to give him a free passage. Once safely in France, he made his way gradually to the region of Auxerre, where some of his mothers relatives lived. He was determined on one thing. Somehow, at some time, he would return to Ireland to bring the faith of Christ to that pagan land ruled in tyranny by the superstitious Druids. But Patrick, though he had great experience of life, had no learning, and he knew before he could be a priest he had a long training before him.

Many years later, after he was a priest, and after a visit to Britain with Saint Germain, Patrick was sent to Rome to discuss with the Pope the possibility of a mission to Ireland. The Pope agreed, entrusted it to Patrick, to whom he gave the special title 'Patercuis,' foreseeing that he would be pater civium – father of his country – and sent him back to Auxerre to make preparations for the mission.

It was probably in the summer of the year 432 that Patrick, now made a bishop, set sail, and landed not far from Wicklow. He determined that the first thing he must do was to find his old master, Milcho, to pay the price of his ransom, and to convert him, who had been cruel, to the religion of the love of Christ. But as he approached Slemish he saw in the distance a great fire raging in Milcho's fort. The chieftain had heard of his coming and of his power to do miracles and, in a frenzy of rage, had gathered all his possessions together in his house, set it on fire, and thrown himself into the flames, because, "his pride could not endure the thought of being vanquished by his former slave."

From one of the chieftains named Dichu, whom he had converted on his way to Slemish, Patrick learned that all the chiefs of Ireland had been summoned by the Supreme King, Laoghaire, to a feast at Tara, where a fire was to be lighted by the Druids as part of the pagan Spring Festival. The day before, all other lights had to be put out and not relighted until the 'sacred fire' blazed out on the royal hill.

The Saints

At the opposite end of the valley to the hill of Tara was the Hill of Slane, and it was here that Patrick and his companions arrived on Easter Eve – for the pagan Spring Festival was on the same day as the Christian Easter. (In that particular year Easter Eve was also the feast of the Annunciation.) Patrick went up to the top of the Hill Slane, and there kindled the Easter fire. When the Druids on Tara saw it they said to King Laoghaire: "This fire which has been lighted in defiance of the royal edict will blaze for ever in this land unless it is put out at once, this very night."

So the King and the Druids and the people all rushed towards the fire, and tried by every means to put it out, and to kill Patrick. But nothing would extinguish the flame, and Patrick, who stood by it singing: "Let God arise and let his enemies be scattered," was preserved from all hurt.

Next day, at the King's invitation, Patrick went to Tara to tell him of the Christian religion. He knew that there was an ambush to try and kill him on the way, and it was on this occasion, that he composed and sang the hymn which is still known as Saint Patrick's Breastplate, which begins: "I bind upon myself today the strong Name of the Trinity," and ends with these words:

> Christ be with me, Christ within me,
> Christ behind me, Christ before me,
> Christ beside me, Christ to win me,
> Christ to comfort and restore me
> Christ beneath me, Christ above me,
> Christ in quiet, Christ in danger,
> Christ in hearts of all that love me,
> Christ in mouth of friend and stranger.

In spite of the ambush, Patrick arrived safely, and after preaching and working signs of wonders before the King, he converted him to the Christian faith, and gained his permission to preach the Gospel throughout the entire land. It was on this day, so men say, that in order to explain to the King the doctrine of the Trinity – how there could be three persons in one God - he picked a shamrock-leaf and drew the lessons from its three petals.

St Patrick is rightly called 'the Apostle of Ireland.' Today we think of him so in the connection with Ireland that we sometimes forget how much he belongs to Christendom - brought up in Britain by his Roman father, who was a Christian, and receiving his training from the great French saint, Germain.

Question 10 ❖ What was the name of the famous hymn composed by Saint Patrick?
Question 11 ❖ Of which country is Saint Patrick the patron?
Question 12 ❖ Which great Saint was baptized by Saint Ambrose?

Level 5 - Lesson 2

Confirmation

The Precepts of the Church

God's Will is made known to us not only through the Ten Commandments, but through the Six Precepts of the Church. These precepts have been studied in earlier levels, but form a part of the knowledge necessary for one to be confirmed. You must remember that a person preparing for the Sacrament of Confirmation, is preparing to become a soldier of Christ, and therefore needs to be well armed with knowledge of his faith.

The Precepts of the Church are:

1) To hear Mass on Sundays and holy days of obligation
2) To fast and abstain on the days appointed
3) To confess our sins at least once a year
4) To receive Holy Communion during Easter time
5) To contribute to the support of the Church
6) To observe the laws of the Church concerning marriage

Traditional Holy Days of Obligation in Australia:

December 25th	Christmas Day
January 1st	The Circumcision
Ascension Thursday	40 days after Easter
August 15th	The Assumption of the Blessed Virgin Mary
November 1st	All Saints' Day

Question 13 ❖ How many traditional holy days of obligation are there in Australia?
Question 14 ❖ Which precepts of the Church apply to school aged children?
Question 15 ❖ Which of the Ten Commandments are directly related to one's neighbor?

Church History

The First Years of Christianity

The First Century (continued)

Before the death of the twelve Apostles the Gospel of Jesus Christ had been preached throughout the greater part of the Roman Empire. Saint Paul, in a letter to the Romans in about 58AD could say that the Faith was 'spoken of in the whole world (Roman)'. At the beginning of the second century (100) in a letter to the Roman Emperor Trajan, Pliny (Governor of Bithynia), said Christians were so numerous in the Province that the old temples and sacrifices were abandoned.

The rapid spread of Christianity in the first century is proof of its Divine origin. Christianity was completely opposed to the religious, social, and political principles and conduct of the people of the time. Religion for them meant worship of false gods, - of idols. Social life was one of immorality and vice. Political life depended on slavery and corruption.

Christianity required purity and holiness of heart and conduct, service of the one true God, obedience to His Ten Commandments.

Pagan people were forced to take notice of the new teachings of Christianity when they saw that Christians were even ready to die for their Faith. They saw the rich and poor, noblemen and slaves, boys and girls, go to their death with joy in their hearts for the love of Jesus Christ.

No man did more to spread the Christian Faith in the First Century than did the great Apostle Saint Paul. In three great missionary journeys through Asia Minor and Greece, Saint Paul visited cities, founded many churches, worked many miracles, ordained many Priests and Bishops, men like Titus and Timothy. Saint Luke, who often traveled with Saint Paul, wrote of Saint Paul's journeys in 'The Acts of the Apostles'. Nor did Saint Paul forget his converts. He wrote many beautiful letters to them, which are now part of the New Testament in the Bible.

Finally Saint Paul was taken prisoner and sent for trial to Rome. On the way he was shipwrecked on Malta. While there he converted the island of Malta to the Faith of Jesus Christ. In Rome Saint Paul was put in jail. A soldier watched over him, chained to him. He was put to death on the same day as Saint Peter in 67AD.

Saint Paul is called the Apostle of the Gentiles, and there is good reason for that title. At first the Apostles preached only to Jews. It was thought converts to Christianity should come through the Jewish religion first. But in a vision given to Saint Peter, related in the Tenth Chapter of the Acts of the Apostles, it was made clear that converts were not restricted to the Jews. Saint Paul preached mainly to Gentiles, not to Jews.

Level 5 - Lesson 2

Church History

At the first Council of Jerusalem 51AD, presided over by Saint Peter, it was decided to open wide the doors of the Church to all peoples, Jews and Gentiles alike.

For the first three hundred years of the Church's life she suffered great persecutions. Thirty of the first thirty-one Popes died Martyrs for the Faith. Countless others shed their blood as Martyrs for Jesus Christ.

Question 16 ◆ When was the first Council of Jerusalem and what did it decree?
Question 17 ◆ Where and when were Saints Peter and Paul put to death?
Question 18 ◆ What was Saul's name after he was converted?

Lesson 3

Level 5

Confirmation

Catechism

The Doctrine of the Incarnation

44. **How many natures has Jesus Christ?**

    Jesus Christ has two natures: the nature of God and the nature of man. (A nature is what someone is, A person is who someone is).

45. **When was Christ born?**

    Christ was born of the Blessed Virgin Mary on Christmas Day, in Bethlehem, more than two thousand years ago.

45a **What is meant by the Incarnation?**

    By the Incarnation is meant that the Son of God, retaining His Divine nature, took to Himself a human nature, that is, a body and soul like ours.

45b **How was the Son of God made man?**

    The Son of God was conceived and made man by the power of the Holy Ghost in the womb of the Blessed Virgin Mary.

Our Lord Jesus Christ is the only person in the history of the world whose appearance on the Earth was foretold repeatedly for thousands of years. From the time of Adam and Eve, until His birth in the stable at Bethlehem, the world awaited Jesus Christ. He is our Saviour, our God, while at the same time He is a man. It is a mystery of our faith, and the Incarnation (becoming flesh) is an essential doctrine of the Catholic Church.

Question 1 ❖ What is meant by the Incarnation?
Question 2 ❖ How many natures has Jesus Christ?
Question 3 ❖ What is the chief teaching of the Catholic Church about Jesus Christ?

Prayer

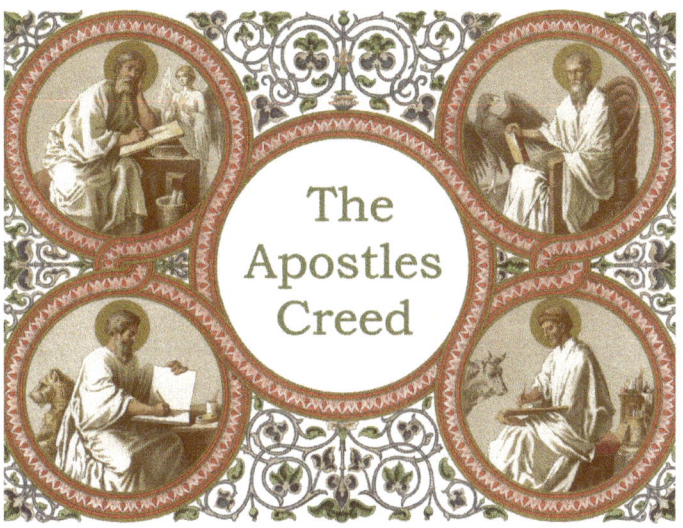

He ascended into Heaven, sitteth at the right hand of God, the Father Almighty;

The sixth article of the Apostles' Creed shows that after His earthly life, He returned to His Father in heaven, sitting at His right hand, showing His equality with the Father, reminding us at the same time that God is indeed, almighty.

From thence He shall come to judge the living and the dead;

It is from the throne of God in heaven, that Our Lord will return at the end of the world to judge all souls, living and death. It will be the moment of God's judgement, even the elect (those saved) will tremble.

Question 4 ❖ How does the Apostles' Creed tell us that the Father and Son are equal?
Question 5 ❖ Who will judge the living and the dead and from whence will He come?
Question 6 ❖ Why is it important to affirm that Jesus really died?

Bible Studies

The Twelve Apostles in Prison – Gamaliel's Counsel

The apostles wrought many signs and wonders among the people. The sick were brought forth into the streets on beds or couches, so that at least the shadow of Peter might fall upon them, and they might be cured. By the daily repetition of these prodigies, the number of believers was wonderfully increased, this gained the attention of the high-priest and he ordered all the twelve apostles to be seized and cast into prison.

But an angel of the Lord came by night, and opening the doors of the prison, led them forth saying: "Go, and, standing, speak in the temple to the people the words of life!" Hearing this, they went into the temple, at the dawn of day, and taught. The chief-priests were enraged when they heard that the apostles were again teaching in the temple.

They gave orders to have them immediately arrested and put into prison. Then the apostles were again brought before the council, and the elders said: "We commanded you that you should not teach in this name. Behold, you have filled Jerusalem with your doctrine." Peter and the apostles answered: "We ought to obey God rather than men. The God of our fathers hath raised up Jesus, whom you put to death, hanging Him on a tree.

"This Prince and Saviour, God hath exalted with His right hand, to give penitence to Israel, and remission of sins." When the priests and ancients heard these things they were filled with anger, and thought to put the apostles to death. But one of the council, a Pharisee named Gamaliel, a doctor of the law, and respected by all the people, rising up, commanded the men to be removed for a little while.

He then addressed the council, saying: "Ye men of Israel, consider with yourselves what you are about to do with these men. If this work be of men, it will fall to nothing. But if it be of God, you are not able to destroy it, lest, perhaps, you be found to oppose God." They agreed with Gamaliel, and calling in the apostles, they scourged them, and charged them to speak no more in the name of Jesus.

But the apostles went forth from the presence of the council rejoicing that they were accounted worthy to suffer torture for the name of Jesus. They went daily to the temple, and from house to house, teaching and preaching to the people, proclaiming everywhere the glory and power of the crucified Saviour of the world.

Question 7   Why did the followers of Christ increase so quickly?
Question 8   How did Peter and the Apostles answer the chief priests when accused of spreading false doctrine?
Question 9   What lesson should we learn from the story of Ananias and Saphira?

Level 5 - Lesson 3

The Saints

Saint Columba

The little Irish prince was christened Colum, which means 'a dove.' As he grew up he became very strong and tall, and every one who saw him said he looked like an angel. He took no part in the fierce fighting of the clans, but when he was quite young he decided to be a priest and to build monasteries, where men could live together in peace, praising God, teaching the people, and going out into the country around telling the pagans about Jesus Christ.

Many of these monasteries he founded in Ireland, and then one day a sad thing happened. There was a quarrel between the tribes which led to fighting and bloodshed, and in some way Columba - the 'dove' - had something to do with it. We do not know exactly what it was, but, as a prince who was fond of his own people, he may have taken sides and forgotten for a moment his duty as a priest. Whatever it was, he was terribly sorry for it, and to show how great his sorrow he determined to do for the love of God the most difficult thing he could think of. He would leave the land and the friends he loved so much and go over the sea to Scotland, where away in the north, were the wild Pict's who had never heard of Christ.

So one day, with twelve friends who were monks like himself, he set sail in a boat made of wickerwork covered with skins of animals – a coracle – called the Dewy Red. They took with them a few provisions to last them until they got to the other side, but, although they were going among fierce men, they took no weapons. They were in long robes of white wool, with nothing but sandals on their feet.

At last they reached one of the islands just off the coast of Scotland and landed on it. Columba looked back over the sea, and there, far away, he could just see the shores of Ireland. "We cannot stay here," said Columba. "We must get in our boat again and go farther on."
"Why must we do that?" asked his companions. "This seems like a good island to build our monastery on." "It is a good island," said Columba, "but we must go on farther because from here we can still see our home. If day by day we look at it over the sea our hearts will always be going back there. Let us go where we cannot see it, and then we shall be more content to live among strangers in a strange land."

So they got out their coracle again and went farther on, till they came to another island which was called Hy, but which is now called Iona. They scrambled on to the shore and looked back over the sea. But this time they could see nothing but waves. The shores of Ireland had disappeared in the distance. "This is our island, surely?" said the monks. "We must make quite sure," said Columba. "Let us climb to the very highest part of the island, for we might be able to see home from there." But even from the top of the highest hill they could see nothing, so there they decided to stay. On the hill they made a little pile of stones, called a cairn, and they named it Carn-cul-ri-Erin, which means the Cairn of the Back-turned-to-Ireland. And on Iona they stayed and built their first monastery.

The Saints

It was their outpost in a new land, and from it these soldiers of Christ made their expeditions into the wild pagan country around. The King of the Pict's Brude, lived far away at Inverness, surrounded by dark forests where wild animals still roamed, and by unknown mountains and glens and lochs. There was no road, and even the Roman soldiers had not been able to push their way through. But Columba and his white-robed monks managed to get there.

They took, of course, a long time on their journey, and by the time they got to Brude's palace the King had heard from his people that they were coming, and had barred the gates against them. Fierce Pictish warriors guarded the gates, ready to fight the newcomers if they were attacked. But the monks carried no weapons; only their staves to help them in the journey – and a wooden Cross. Columba walked straight up to the bolted and barred gates and, raising his hand, made the sign of the Cross upon it. Immediately, of its own accord, it opened and swung wide. The guards ran away in terror to tell the King what had happened. They thought that Columba must be some powerful magician. But King Brude was not frightened. He left the heathen priests who were with him and came and welcomed Columba, and asked him to tell him who he was, and why he had come to see him. So Columba told him about Jesus Christ, and how he had journeyed so far to bring him the Good News of the Gospel. The two became great friends.

When Columba got back to Iona he found that there were many other places to which he could send missionaries. His monks went out all over Scotland, and even into England, preaching; and more and more people came to Iona to help him.

In those days all books had to be written by hand, and Columba himself made copies of the Gospels and the Psalms to send out by his missionaries. One night as he was working in this way he grew very tired, and he knew that he had not long to live. He was seventy-six years old, and his life had not been easy. When he got to the verse, "They who seek the Lord shall want no manner of thing that is good," he said to those round him, "Here I must stop. Others must write what follows." It was a Saturday morning when he told them, "This is the last day of my life of labor on earth; at midnight, when the solemn Day of the Lord begins, I shall go the way of my fathers."

Through that night he sat up in his cell, where he had a bare rock for a mattress and a stone for a pillow, and as the bell rang for Matins he went into the church. Dermot, one of the monks, followed quickly and called, "Where are you, Father?" It was quite dark, for the lamps had not yet been brought in, and he could not see Columba. Nor was there any answer. Groping his way, he found Columba lying on the altar steps, unable to speak.

Meanwhile the other monks had come in with lights, and when they were all there Columba managed to move his hand a little, and they knew that he was giving them his last blessing. Then he died, but his face was so happy and peaceful that he seemed to be living and sleeping. They buried him in Iona, but years later, when the Danes started their invasions, burning churches and monasteries, the body of Columba was taken for safety across the sea back to the Ireland he had loved and left.

Question 10 ❖ What type of Apostolate was that of Saint Columba?
Question 11 ❖ What did Saint Columba do to make King Brude his friend?
Question 12 ❖ What was the name of the famous hymn composed by Saint Patrick?

Level 5 - Lesson 3

Confirmation

The Divine Institution of Confirmation

1) When was Confirmation instituted? The exact time at which Confirmation was instituted is not known. It is certain that Christ instituted this Sacrament and instructed His Apostles in its use at some time before His Ascension into heaven.

2) What promise did Christ make before He left this earth? He promised the guidance of the Holy Ghost, the Third Person of the Trinity, the "Spirit of Truth" Whom He would send to teach them all things whatsoever He had told them. "I will ask the Father, and He shall give you another Paraclete, that He may abide with you forever" (John 14:16). "You shall receive the power of the Holy Ghost coming upon you" (Acts 1:8).

3) Did Our Lord keep His promise? Yes, ten days after His Ascension He sent the Holy Ghost down upon the Apostles in the form of tongues of fire. "Suddenly there came a sound from heaven, as of a mighty wind coming, and it filled the whole house where they were sitting. And there appeared to them parted tongues as it were of fire, and it sat upon every one of them. And they were filled with the Holy Ghost; and they began to speak with diverse tongues according as the Holy Ghost gave them to speak (Acts 2:2).

4) What effects did the descent of the Holy Ghost have upon the Apostles? The Apostles were truly confirmed, that is to say, strengthened; their understanding was fully penetrated with the whole and entire doctrine of Divine Faith; their minds clearly grasped the Divine truths; their will was entirely under His sway so that they fearlessly preached the Gospel to the whole world.

5) What effects did the descent of the Holy Ghost have upon the early Christians? They received a special assistance to enable them to undergo great afflictions and severe trials on account of their new faith.

6) What commission did Our Lord give the Apostles? He commanded them to confer the Holy Ghost by the imposition of hands on all who were properly disposed to receive the sacrament of Confirmation. "As the Father hath sent Me, I also send you" (John 20:21).

7) Does the Church still practice the ancient custom of imposing hands to call down the Holy Ghost upon those who have been baptized? Yes, the Church still possesses and dispenses the graces of the Holy Ghost in a special sacrament by the imposition of hands through the ministry of the bishops to the faithful after Baptism.

Question 13 ❖ What was the promise of Christ before He left this earth?
Question 14 ❖ What command did Our Lord give to the Apostles?
Question 15 ❖ Which precepts of the Church apply to school aged children?

Church History

The First Century

In the early days of the Church, Jewish Priests and people, even some Apostles, were opposed to the preaching of the Gospel of Jesus to the Gentiles or non-Jews. It was decided at the First Council of Jerusalem to throw the Church wide open to all converts, Jews or Gentiles alike.

All opposition from the Jews to Gentile converts ended with the punishment prophesied by Jesus, which came upon them in the year 70AD. In 66AD some Jews revolted against Roman authority. Vespasian, a Roman soldier was sent by the Emperor to crush the rebellion. In 68AD Vespasian himself became Emperor of Rome. He sent his son Titus against the Jews. Titus laid siege to Jerusalem and destroyed the city in 70AD. Thousands of Jews died, thousands were sold as slaves, the Temple was destroyed. The Jews were driven forth to wander as strangers and outcasts in every land.

The religion of the Jews, Judaism, now lost all its influence, and the Church had no more trouble from the Jews. But there was far worse trouble in store for the Church, for she now found herself opposed by the whole Roman Empire.

The Romans were pagans, they worshiped false gods; immorality and vice were everywhere. The Emperor was worshiped as a god. The slaves had no rights and could be treated in any manner. The Church condemned the idolatry of Rome, its immorality and vice; it taught that slaves also had souls redeemed by Christ. Because the Church refused to worship the Emperor as God, Christians were pronounced guilty of treason.

The Christian Church boldly condemned all the evils of the Roman Empire, and the Roman Empire then turned on the Christian Church in terrible anger.

For about 250 years the Roman Empire tried her best to crush and destroy the Christian Church. There were only short periods of peace for Christians between the years 68 and 300AD. In that time no fewer than ten of the Roman Emperors used all the power of the Empire in vain attempts to wipe out the Church.

During the latter half of the First Century there was the terrible persecution by the Emperor Nero (54 - 68AD). It began in the year 64AD. Christians suffered many tortures. They were drowned, exposed to the wild beasts, crucified and burnt to death.

Among the Martyrs of Nero were Saints Peter and Paul. In the Year 67AD Saint Peter was crucified upside down and Saint Paul was beheaded. Before the end of the First Century there was the persecution of Emperor Domitian. In the year 95AD, the Apostle Saint John was thrown into boiling oil. By a miracle he was saved. Saint John was banished to the Isle of Patmos in the Aegean Sea. There he wrote the Apocalypse, the last book of the Bible.

So the First Century ended with a Church suffering great persecution.

Question 16 ❖ What happened in the Year 70AD?
Question 17 ❖ What came after the Jewish persecutions?
Question 18 ❖ Which Emperor led the first great persecution in 64AD?
Question 19 ❖ When was the first Council of Jerusalem and what did it decree?

Lesson 4

Level 5

Confirmation

Catechism

The Doctrine of the Incarnation

45c   **On what day did the Son of God become man?**

The Son of God became man on the twenty-fifth of March, the day of the Annunciation.

45d   **Is Saint Joseph the father of Jesus Christ?**

Jesus Christ has no human father, but Saint Joseph was the spouse of the Blessed Virgin Mary and the guardian, or foster father of Jesus Christ.

45e   **What is a supernatural mystery?**

A supernatural mystery is a truth we cannot fully understand, but which we firmly believe because we have God's word for it.

When we don't understand something, we often think it is either wrong, or silly! Because we don't understand it, that does not make it wrong, or make it silly. It means we do not understand it. It is a mystery! Do you understand how electricity works? If not, it is a mystery to you, yet you believe it exists. A supernatural mystery cannot be fully understood by us, but we believe it because God has revealed it to us. Jesus Himself said to Saint Thomas, "Blessed are they who do not see, but believe".

Question 1 ❖ Is Saint Joseph the father of Jesus Christ?
Question 2 ❖ What is a supernatural mystery?
Question 3 ❖ How many natures has Jesus Christ?

Level 5 - Lesson 4

Prayer

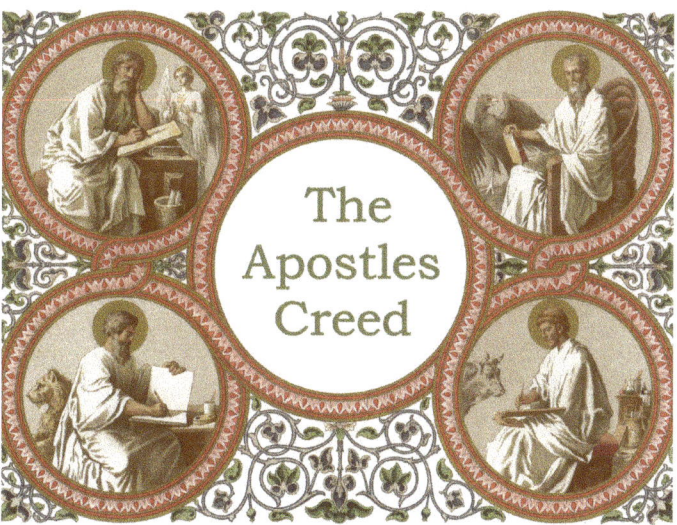

I believe in the Holy Ghost

We have already professed our belief in the first two Persons of the Blessed Trinity, and now we demonstrate our belief in the Holy Ghost, the Third Person of the Blessed Trinity.

The Holy Catholic Church; the Communion of Saints

To believe in God, one must believe in what He has taught us or in what He has decreed. God, through the Second Person of the Blessed Trinity, founded a Church, the Holy Catholic Church. We are therefore bound to follow that Church as it comes from God.

The Communion of Saints is the Church Militant (the Church on Earth), the Church Suffering (the Church in Purgatory) and the Church Triumphant (the Church in Heaven). This Communion of souls (saints) help one another, by prayers and/or sufferings. Thus, we can pray to the saints in Heaven or to the poor souls in Purgatory. Likewise we can help the poor souls by our prayers and sacrifices.

Question 4	❖	How many persons are there in the Blessed Trinity and what are their names?
Question 5	❖	What is meant by the Communion of Saints?
Question 6	❖	Who will judge the living and the dead and from whence will He come?

Bible Studies

The Election of the Deacons – Stephen the First Martyr

As the number of the disciples increased, it happened that some poor widows were neglected in the daily distribution. Therefore it was that the apostles, calling together the multitude of the disciples, said: "It is not fit that we should leave the word of God, and serve tables. Therefore, brethren, look out among you seven men of good reputation, full of the Holy Ghost and wisdom, whom we may appoint over this business."

This proposal was pleasing to the disciples. They chose Stephen, a man full of faith and of the Holy Ghost, with Philip and five others. These they presented to the apostles, who prayed over them, and imposed hands upon them. Stephen, full of grace and power, did great wonders amongst the people. Some of the most learned of the doctors, envying his fame, began to dispute with him, but even they could not equal the marvelous wisdom with which he spoke.

Ashamed of their defeat, they stirred up the people against him. He was seized and brought before the council. They then brought up false witnesses, who testified that he ceased not to speak against the holy place and the law. All the members of the council looked angrily upon him, but they saw his face shining like that of an angel. Filled with divine love and the Spirit of God, Stephen reminded them of the wonders which God had wrought for their fathers in Egypt and other places.

After showing them how ungrateful their fathers had been, he concluded with these words: "With a stiff neck and uncircumcised heart and ears, you always resist the Holy Ghost, as your fathers did. Which of the prophets have not your fathers persecuted? And they have slain those who foretold the coming of the Just One, of whom you have been now betrayers and murderers!" When they heard him speak like this, they raged, and gnashed their teeth with fury. But Stephen, being filled with the Holy Ghost, looked up steadfastly into heaven, and saw the glory of God, and Jesus standing at the right hand of God. When Stephen told them of his vision, they cried out with a loud voice and stopped their ears, and rushing upon him with one accord, drove him out of the city, and stoned him.

Whilst Stephen was being put to death, a young man named Saul held the garments of the murderers. But Stephen, falling on his knees, cried with a loud voice: "Lord, lay not this sin to their charge!" When he had said these words, he died. The prayer of Saint Stephen for his enemies was very pleasing to God, and some say that through this prayer, Saul received, later on, the grace of conversion.

Question 7 ◆ Why were seven men chosen to help the Apostles?
Question 8 ◆ Who was the first martyr and how did he die?
Question 9 ◆ Why did the followers of Christ increase so quickly?

Level 5 - Lesson 4

The Saints

Saint Gregory VII

The Pope of the 'Investiture Contest,' Gregory VII, like Gregory the Great, five hundred years earlier, was also a monk in a Benedictine monastery, and was called upon to defend the Church. His name was Hildebrand, and he was the son of a carpenter of Sovana. He was not very tall; spoke with a stammer; and the only remarkable thing people could see about him was his glittering bright eyes which made them say that he was like his name, which means 'a bright flame.'

The times in which he lived were bad ones for the Church. People said that it seemed as if Christ were asleep and His vessel, the Church, tossed about at the mercy of the storm. One man wrote, "The whole world lay in wickedness; holiness had disappeared; justice had perished; and truth had been buried." The worst of it was that the wickedness of the world had got inside the Church itself. Monasteries had fallen into ruin; priests no longer looked after their people; bishops only cared for money and land and luxury. Hildebrand saw that one of the reasons for this was that the kings and princes of Europe insisted that every bishop should pay homage to them, just as if they were ordinary nobles. They, and not the Pope or his representatives, gave the new bishop the crosier – the 'shepherd's crook,' which showed that he was to obey Jesus' command, "Feed my sheep" - and the ring, which showed his 'marriage' to the Church. These things, of course, should never have been given by anyone who was not himself a representative of Christ's Church; but the kings and princes refused to give up the right of 'investiture,' as it was called. So the wrong kind of men became bishops, and the whole Church suffered.

When Hildebrand became Pope he said that this must stop. He turned out the bishops who had allowed a lay man to 'invest' them, and he said that any ruler who continued to do this should not be allowed to take Holy Communion. Even the most powerful of all the rulers, Henry, the Emperor, who ruled over what is now Germany and parts of Italy, was excommunicated. When Henry prepared to fight rather than obey, the Pope pronounced him deposed. "For the honor and security of the Church, in the name of God Almighty, I prohibit Henry, who has risen against the Church, from ruling Germany and Italy. I release all Christians from the oaths of fidelity they may have taken to him, and I order that no one shall obey him."

At first Henry did not take much notice, but when some of his own people like Saint Benno were turning against him in Germany he thought he had better make friends with the Pope and get him to forgive him. So he set out on a journey to Italy, secretly hoping that, even if the Pope remained hard, some Italians would come over to his side.

It was in the middle of winter, and Gregory was in a castle called Canossa, far up in the mountains. Henry, finding that the Italians would not fight for him, made the long journey there through the snow. But when he arrived the Pope refused to see him. "If the King is truly sorry," he said, "let him surrender his crown and sceptre to me to prove it."

The Saints

But in the end he allowed Henry, after he had kept him waiting in the castle yard for three days, barefoot, fasting, and clothed like a penitent, to see him. Henry threw himself at Gregory's feet, crying, "Holy Father, spare me," and was immediately forgiven.

Gregory had insisted on this, not, of course, because he did not like Henry, but because he wanted to give everyone in Europe a lesson that the power of the Church, because it is founded by Christ, is more important than earthly power at all. And in your history books you will still read about Canossa, which happened just eleven years after the battle of Hastings was won in England by one of Gregory's friends, William the Conqueror.

Though Henry pretended to be sorry, he was not so really. He went away again, broke all his promises, raised a great army, and drove Gregory out of Rome. The Saint's last words as he died in exile at Spoleto were, "Because I have loved righteousness and hated iniquity, therefore I die in exile." But in the years to come it was his cause, not Henry's, which was victorious.

Question 10 ❖ Which great king did Saint Gregory VII excommunicate?
Question 11 ❖ What was meant by 'investiture'?
Question 12 ❖ What type of Apostolate was that of Saint Columba?

Level 5 - Lesson 4

Confirmation

Nature of Confirmation

1) What is Confirmation?
   Confirmation is a sacrament of the New Law, instituted by Our Lord Jesus Christ, which strengthens the divine life in us, and gives to those who are baptized the Holy Ghost with all His gifts.

2) Why is it called Confirmation?
   Because this sacrament strengthens and perfects the new life which the grace of Jesus Christ bestows in Baptism.

3) What are some of the names given by the Fathers of the Church to the sacrament of Confirmation?
   1) Imposition of hands.
   2) The Sacrament of Holy Chrism.
   3) The Seal of Our Lord.
   4) The Spiritual Seal.
   5) The Sign by which the Holy Ghost is received.

4) Why is Confirmation a true sacrament?
   Because it has all the conditions that are required for a sacrament.

   1) An outward sign.
   2) An inward grace.
   3) The institution by Jesus Christ.

5) What is the outward sign of Confirmation?
   It is the visible action by which the sacrament is administered, and consists of matter and form, which signify the grace to be conferred.

6) What are the matter and form of Confirmation?
   1) The matter of the sacrament consists in the laying of the bishop's hands, and the anointing with chrism.

   2) The form consists in the sacred words pronounced by the bishop, which express the receiving of the Holy Ghost and the sealing of the soul in Jesus Christ.

7) What is Holy Chrism? What does the oil signify?
   1) The Holy Chrism is composed of olive oil and fragrant balsam blessed by the bishop on Holy Thursday.

   2) The oil signifies the inward strength conferred upon the soul by the Holy Ghost.

Confirmation

8) What does the balsam mixed with oil signify?

Balsam is mixed with oil when it is consecrated by the bishop to signify that he who is to be confirmed receives the grace to keep himself free from sinful corruption and to send forth the sweet odor of a holy life.

9) What does the bishop say when he consecrates the chrism?

"God grant this virtue to the chrism of the Holy Ghost, that by the sanctification infused by chrism, the corruption of the first birth may be absorbed, the holy temple of each one may breathe the lovely odor of an innocent life."

10) Is Confirmation necessary for salvation?

Confirmation is not, like Baptism, absolutely necessary for salvation. But all Catholics ought to receive it if they have the opportunity, as it confers sacramental grace.

11) Is it a sin to neglect Confirmation?

It is a sin to neglect Confirmation, especially in these days when faith and morals are exposed to so many and such violent temptations.

Question 13 ❖ What are the matter and form of Confirmation?
Question 14 ❖ Is Confirmation necessary for salvation?
Question 15 ❖ What was the promise of Christ before He left this earth?

Level 5 - Lesson 4

Church History

Persecutions

The next great persecution of the Church began under Emperor Trajan. He returned to Rome in 105 after winning many battles against Rome's enemies. The Christians refused to join in his pagan victory celebrations. The persecution then began. It was very severe in Asia Minor.

Saint Ignatius, Bishop of Antioch, was sent to Rome and was thrown to the lions in the Colosseum in 107. The most violent persecution of Christians was that begun by the Emperor Decius in 249. Christians were killed in their thousands in every part of the Empire. Every form of torture was used. A great many Bishops and Priests were put to death. This great persecution was carried on after Decius, by the Emperor Valerian who reigned 253 – 260. Pope Saint Stephen was martyred, as was Pope Saint Sixtus II. Among four Deacons who were martyred was Saint Laurence. He was roasted over a fire. The last general persecution of the Church began under the Emperor Diocletian in 300. Rewards were promised to those who denied their faith. Those who remained true to their faith were tortured and killed. Martyrs of this persecution were Saint Agnes, Saint Sebastian, and the boy Saint Pancratius. In Switzerland Saint Maurice, Captain of the Theban Legion, and all his fellow Christian soldiers were killed.

In spite of all these persecutions, Christianity continued to spread rapidly. So true is it to say that the blood of the Martyrs is the seed of the Church. The Emperor Diocletian retired in 305, and later starved himself to death. There followed some years of confusion over the successor to Diocletian, but at length Constantine the Great succeeded and became Emperor of Rome. Constantine's mother, Saint Helena, was a British Princess and already a fervent Christian. From her, Constantine learned much about the Christian Faith.

In 312 Constantine defeated his rival to the throne at Milvian Bridge near Rome. Before the battle Constantine had seen a vision in the sky of a cross with the words, 'In this sign you shall conquer.' He had a battle standard made like the vision, and with this standard carried at the head of his troops, Constantine won a great victory. In 313 Constantine published from Milan the 'EDICT OF MILAN'. This gave freedom and toleration to all Christians. Soon after that Constantine declared himself to be a Christian. After two and a half centuries of persecution, the Church was free. The Cross replaced the Eagle on the standards of Rome

Question 16 ❖ How was Saint Ignatius of Antioch martyred?
Question 17 ❖ Which Emperor led the last general persecution of the Church?
Question 18 ❖ Who published the Edict of Milan and what was it?
Question 19 ❖ What happened in the Year 70AD?

Lesson 5

Level 5

Confirmation

Catechism

The Doctrine of the Redemption

46. What is meant by the redemption?

By the redemption is meant that Jesus Christ offered His sufferings and death to God in satisfaction for the sins of men.

47. What do we learn from the sufferings and death of Christ?

From the sufferings and death of Christ we learn God's love for man and the evil of sin.

48. What do we mean when we say in the Apostles' Creed that Christ descended into hell?

When we say that Christ descended into hell we mean that, after He died, the soul of Christ descended into a place or state of rest, called limbo, where the souls of the just were waiting for Him.

49. When did Christ rise from the dead?

Christ rose from the dead, glorious and immortal, on Easter Sunday, the third day after His death.

Our Lord came onto this earth to save us from sin. He redeemed us, that is, He made up for the sin of Adam and made it possible for us to enter heaven one day. He suffered so much on our account.

Whenever we are tempted to be lazy, or to do something that we know is wrong, remember what Our Lord suffered for us.

Question 1 ❖ What is meant by the redemption?
Question 2 ❖ What do we learn from the sufferings and death of Christ?
Question 3 ❖ What is a supernatural mystery?

Prayer

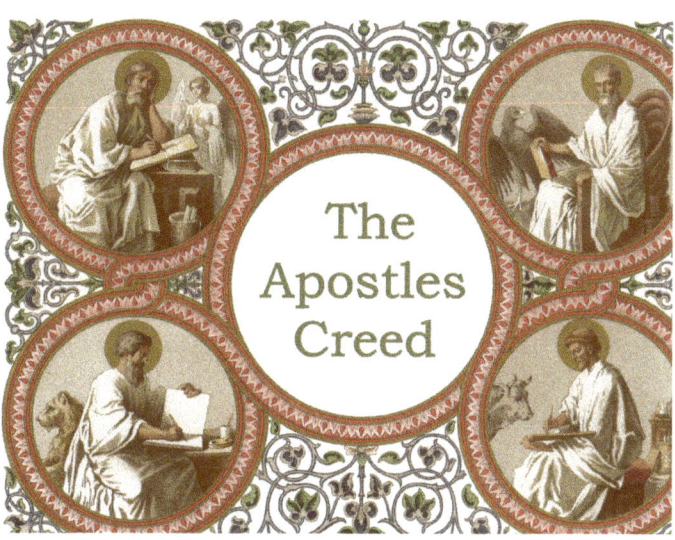

The forgiveness of sins;

As Catholics, we know that no matter how many and how grievous our sins have been, if we are truly sorry for them, through the Sacrament of Penance our sins are washed away and our soul becomes white again. It is a great consolation for us, who are sinners.

The resurrection of the body;

After we die, we are judged. Our soul goes to heaven, hell or purgatory, and our bodies are laid in the ground where they rot. But at the end of the world, our bodies will rise from the mud of the earth, and for those who are in heaven, their souls will reunite with their glorious resurrected bodies. Our bodies will resemble the glory of Our Lord's Body after the Resurrection.

And life everlasting. Amen.

Heaven is eternal. That is, it will last forever. It will have no end. It is difficult for us to understand that our happiness will last forever. We have never experienced such happiness in this world. Imagine a time in your life when you were extremely happy. Now multiply that happiness by a billion. You have not even started to understand the happiness of heaven. Imagine this happiness has lasted for a trillion years (if you can), that trillion years of happiness is not even as much as the first moment of happiness in heaven. If we live a life according to the laws of God, our reward will be everlasting.

Question 4 ❖ What happens to our bodies after we die?
Question 5 ❖ What happens to our bodies at the end of the world?
Question 6 ❖ What do we mean by life everlasting?
Question 7 ❖ What is meant by the Communion of Saints?

Bible Studies

The Sacrament of Confirmation
Baptism of the Officer of Queen Candace

After the death of Stephen, the disciples of Jesus Christ were grievously afflicted in Jerusalem. Among the worst of the persecutors was Saul, the same who had held the garments of those who put Stephen to death. He went from house to house, dragging out men and women who professed to be followers of Christ, and threw them in prison.

On account of this fierce oppression, the disciples were scattered abroad through all Judea and Samaria, preaching everywhere the gospel of Jesus Christ. The deacon Philip went to Samaria, where he cured all manner of diseases. The inhabitants of that city received the gospel with joy, believed and were baptized.

When the apostles in Jerusalem heard this they sent Peter and John to confirm the newly baptized. The two apostles went to Samaria and prayed for the new Christians. Then they imposed hands upon them, and they received the Holy Ghost. After Peter and John had preached the gospel in Samaria, and the country around it, they returned to Jerusalem.

But an angel appeared to Philip, saying: "Arise, and go towards the south, to the way from Jerusalem down to Gaza!" Philip went immediately. While journeying along, he was overtaken on the road by an officer of Candace, Queen of Ethiopia, who was returning from Jerusalem, where he had gone to worship.

As he rode along, sitting in his chariot, he read aloud the prophecy of Isaias. Then the spirit said to Philip: "Go near, and join that chariot!" He did so, and heard the officer reading the words: "As a sheep, He was led to the slaughter; and, like a lamb, without a voice, before His shearer, so opened He not His mouth." Philip asked him: "Do you understand that what you read?" The officer replied: "How can I, unless some one shows me?"

He then requested Philip to come up into the chariot and sit with him. Philip did so, and, beginning with the text which had puzzled the officer, he explained to him all the Scriptures relating to Jesus Christ, instructing him in the mystery of redemption.

As they rode on, they came to a stream, and the stranger said to Philip: "See, here is water, what stops me from being baptized?" Philip replied: "If you believe with thy whole heart, then you may!" He answered: "I believe that Jesus Christ is the Son of God." He then stopped the Chariot, and they both went down into the water, and Philip baptized the officer. But when they came up out of the water, the Spirit of the Lord took away Philip, and the officer saw him no more. Praising and glorifying God, he went back joyfully to his own country.

Question 8 ❖ Why were the apostles scattered abroad through all of Judea and Samaria?
Question 9 ❖ What did Saint Philip explain to the officer of Queen Candace?
Question 10 ❖ Why were seven men chosen to help the Apostles?

Level 5 - Lesson 5

The Saints

Saint Norbert

Norbert, the son of one of the German counts and a relative of the Emperor, was born in Xanten, on the Rhine, in the year 1080. When he was quite young he was given a post at the court of the Emperor, Henry V (whose wife, Matilda, later tried to get the throne of England from King Stephen). Norbert was rich, handsome, and clever, he greatly enjoyed his life as a courtier and cared for nothing but pleasure. But one day when riding not far from Xanten he was caught in a thunderstorm. A thunderbolt actually fell just in front of his horse, which reared and plunged in panic that Norbert was thrown violently to the ground, and it was an hour before his attendants could restore him to consciousness. When he recovered his senses he was a changed man. He realized how near death he had been and what a careless, sinful life he had led, and determined that the future should be quite different.

He placed himself under the guidance of a Benedictine abbot and became a priest. He celebrated his first Mass at Xanten, and at it he preached a sermon reminding men how short life is and how they owe it to God to live it as He wishes. Some of the worldly clergy there were so angry that, it is said, one even spat in his face afterwards. He was not angry with them, but he determined to show them that he himself was prepared to do what he asked other people to do. He sold all his great possessions and gave the money to the poor, keeping for himself only what was needed to celebrate Mass. With a mule to carry the vestments and the sacred vessels, he set out, clothed in a lamb-skin, with a cord round his waist, and barefoot, to go through Germany preaching repentance like a new Saint John the Baptist. He traveled in this way to France, where he turned men from their careless way of living, and to Italy, where he visited the Pope, who wished to keep him at his court. But Norbert would not stay – he was afraid of courts – so the Pope gave him permission to continue his preaching wherever in Europe he found need for it. He offered him the Bishop of Cambrai, but Norbert refused it, because he was sure that he had other work to do for God.

One night he had a dream in which he saw a great meadow in the middle of a forest. In it was a ruined chapel, dedicated to Saint John the Baptist, and there was a procession of white-robed men coming out of it. And it seemed that he was not there by chance but that the Blessed Virgin Mary was herself pointing it out to him. It was, indeed, a vision rather than a dream. Some time later as, with a few companions, he was travelling through the forest of Coucy, he suddenly came upon the spot which he had seen in that vision, and, going to pray in the little chapel, he knew what he had to do. He was to found a new Order in the Church, of men who, like himself, would live in poverty and holiness and call the careless to repentance. He named the place Premontre, which means 'the meadow that was pointed out,' and his new Order, dressed in white woollen cloaks over coarse black habits like those he had seen, was called – as its members still are today – the Premonstratensians. At first he and his companions lived in huts of wood and clay, arranged like a camp round the little chapel, but they soon built a larger church and a monastery to house the people who soon began to join the new Order.

Norbert, as he was travelling to various places to get money and help for Premontre, visited once more the Emperor's court, where some of his old friends remembered him. One of these companions of his youth, seeing him barefoot, ill-dressed, and worn with fasting, said: "Oh, Norbert! That I should live to see you like this!"

The Saints

One of the young chaplains, named Hugh, was much surprised that the courtier should even recognize the beggar, and asked who he was. "That," said the courtier, "was once the cheeriest and most carefree man at court. And if he is now poor and despised it is because he has refused wealth and honors. I have heard that the Bishop of Cambrai was offered to him, but he would not take it." Hugh, who was himself meaning to make a career at court, was so impressed that he joined Norbert, went back with him to Premontre, and became, in time, his second in command.

In the first five years after the founding of the new Order it spread over Europe. Houses were established in Germany and France, and in what are now Holland and Belgium. Norbert decided that he must get the new Pope's blessing on it and authority to continue it, so with Hugh and two other companions he set out for Rome once more. The new Pope confirmed the Order but at the same time gave Norbert other work to do. He was now forty-six years old, and, as the Investiture Contest was still continuing, the authorities in the Church felt the need of Norbert's power and intellect in ruling the German Church. So Norbert, though he did not wish it, was made Bishop of Magdeburg. When he went to Magdeburg to be installed he traveled simply as he always did. He arrived at night when the gates were shut, and when, in answer to the knocking, the porter looked out to see who was there he called roughly: "Away, fellow, we don't want any beggars here." The porter, of course, apologized when he realized that the 'beggar' was the new Prince-Bishop; but there were others in Magdeburg who did not want any interference in their worldly life, such as they felt the saintly Norbert would insist on. And when as Bishop he tried to put things right and return to the poor and the Church the goods and land that had been taken by the powerful and rich men of Magdeburg, three attempts were made to murder him.

Norbert, now at the end of his life as he had been at the beginning, frequently at court as the friend of the Emperor and of the Pope alike, made one last journey to Rome to reconcile them to each other, but his great labors had worn him out. He had to be carried in a litter to Magdeburg, where he died just after Whit-Sunday in 1134 without being able to visit his beloved Premontre again. The effort of the monasteries to become what they were meant to be was made in France as well as in Germany.

Saint Norbert's Feast Day is June 6th

Question 11 ◆ How was Norbert converted?
Question 12 ◆ What religious Order did Saint Norbert start?
Question 13 ◆ Which great king did Saint Gregory VII excommunicate?

Level 5 - Lesson 5

Confirmation

The Minister of Confirmation

1) Who has the power to confirm?
   The power to confirm resides in the bishops of the Church who, succeeding the Apostles, are the ordinary ministers of Confirmation.

2) Who is the extraordinary minister of Confirmation?
   The extraordinary minister of Confirmation is a priest who has received the power by special delegation of the Apostolic See.*
   (*By a decree of September 14, 1946, the Pastor in his own territory may confirm all the faithful who are in danger of death from a serious illness from which it is foreseen they will die.)

3) Can the extraordinary minister consecrate the chrism used in Confirmation?
   No, he must use the chrism which has been consecrated by the bishop.

4) What must an extraordinary minister do before conferring Confirmation?
   He must announce beforehand that while a bishop is the ordinary minister, he himself has a special power from the Holy See to confer the sacrament; and he must use the same rite as the bishop.

5) When may Confirmation be administered?
   Confirmation may be administered at any time of the year, at any hour, even in the evening if the bishop should so arrange.

6) Where does the bishop confirm?
   The proper place of the ceremony is in the Church, but the bishop for a reasonable cause, may confer the sacrament in any becoming place.

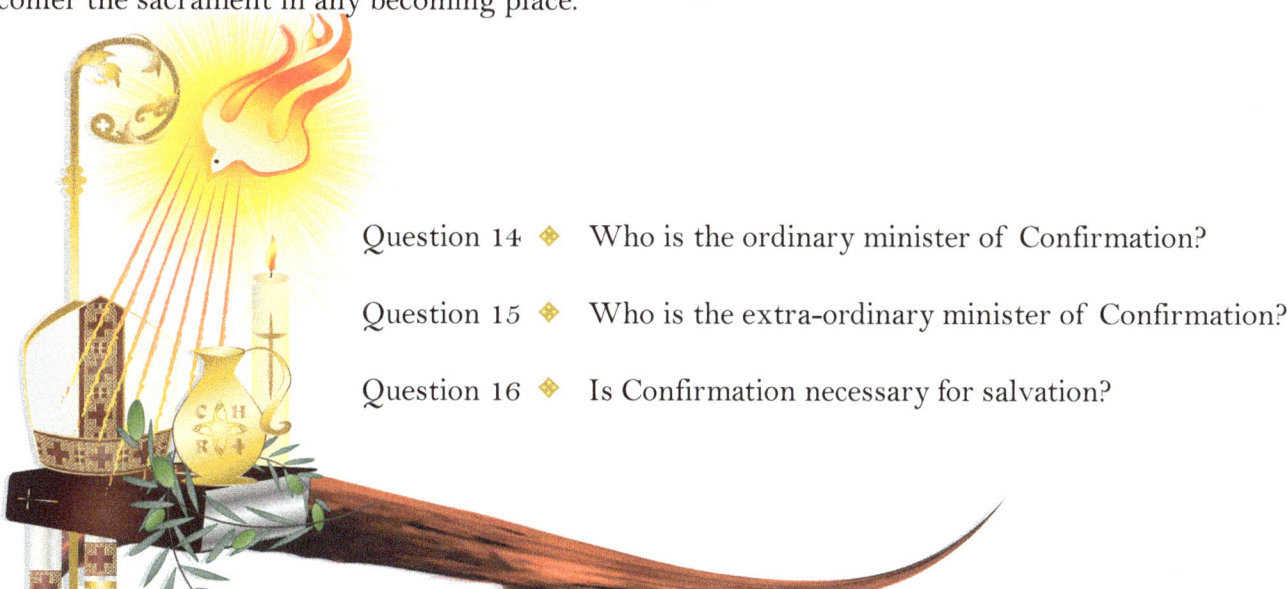

Question 14 ❖ Who is the ordinary minister of Confirmation?

Question 15 ❖ Who is the extra-ordinary minister of Confirmation?

Question 16 ❖ Is Confirmation necessary for salvation?

Church History

Heresies
The Enemy Within

Having survived the persecutions of Rome up to 300AD a new danger threatened the Church for the next 300 years, a danger from within the Church, coming from a succession of heresies.
(Heresy = to deny or reject a doctrine or teaching of the Church.)

The first great heresy was ARIANISM. Arius was a Priest of Alexandria in Egypt, who taught in 318, that the Second Person of the Blessed Trinity was not God, and so inferior to the Father. This led to the denial of the Blessed Trinity, the Incarnation and Redemption.

At first, Constantine favored Arius, but changed his mind and called together a general Council of Bishops of the Church at Nicea, the chief town in Bithynia in Asia Minor. The Council of Nicea was held in 325. The council condemned Arianism, and drew up the Nicene Creed, which defined the doctrine of the Blessed Trinity, the Incarnation and Redemption. This Nicene Creed is said at Mass every Sunday.

The great hero of the Church at the Council of Nicea was Saint Athanasius, who shortly after became the Patriarch of Alexandria. For fifty years Athanasius struggled against Arianism. On five occasions he had to flee into exile from the anger of Arian heretics. Saint Athanasius died in the year 375

In 430 the NESTORIAN heresy began. Nestorius, Bishop of Constantinople, began to teach that there are two persons in Christ, human and divine. He said Mary could not be the Mother of God, but only the Mother of the human person in Christ. Catholic doctrine teaches that there are two natures, human and divine, in the one Person of Jesus Christ, and that Mary is the Mother of God because her Son Jesus Christ, is God. The great opponent of Nestorius was Saint Cyril of Alexandria. Again a General Council of the Church was called to meet at Ephesus in 431.

The Council of Ephesus was presided over by Saint Cyril, Legate of the Pope. It condemned Nestorianism, and gave Mary the title "Mother of God".

Then a priest of Constantinople named Etyches fell into the opposite heresy from Nestorius. He denied that there are two natures, human and divine, in Christ. This heresy was condemned at the Council of Chalcedon in 451.

Catholic doctrine requires that we believe Jesus Christ is both God and Man otherwise He could not atone sufficiently for our sins, nor could He suffer and die for us. In the West the great heresy of this time was PELAGIANISM. Pelagius, a Welshman, denied 'Free will' and hence the Catholic doctrine of Grace and Merit. Saint Augustine, Bishop of Hippo in North Africa, opposed Pelagius. Born in 354, and under the influence of Saint Ambrose, Archbishop of Milan, he was converted and became a Priest, then Bishop of Hippo.

For 34 years Augustine wrote and preached in defense of the Church. He is one of the greatest Doctors of the Church. He died in 430 at the very time the Vandals began to threaten Roman civilization.

Church History

Question 17 ◆ What was the Arian heresy?
Question 18 ◆ Which Saint and which Council of the Church fought the Arian heresy?
Question 19 ◆ What was the Nestorian Heresy?
Question 20 ◆ What was the Pelagian Heresy?
Question 21 ◆ What is meant by the word heresy?
Question 22 ◆ Who published the Edict of Milan and what was it?

Lesson 6

Level 5

Confirmation

Catechism

The Doctrine of the Redemption

50. **When did Christ ascend into heaven?**
Christ ascended, body and soul, into heaven on Ascension Day, forty days after His Resurrection.

51. **What do we mean when we say that Christ sits at the right hand of God, the Father Almighty?**
When we say that Christ sits at the right hand of God, the Father Almighty, we mean that Our Lord as God is equal to the Father, and that as man He has the highest place in heaven, next to God.

52 **What do we mean when we say that Christ will come from thence to judge the living and the dead?**
When we say that Christ will come from thence to judge the living and the dead, we mean that on the last day Our Lord will come to judge everyone who has ever lived in this world.

After Our Lord's Resurrection, He spent forty days more upon our earth appearing to his disciples. On the fortieth day, He left this earth and ascended into heaven where He sits at the right hand of God the Father. Our Lord came onto the earth as a man (Incarnation), suffered and died for us that the sin of Adam might be repaired (Redemption), and now He ascends to His Father in heaven, promising to send us the Holy Ghost, asking us to correspond with His graces that we might be saved.

Question 1 ◈ What do we mean when we say that Christ sits at the right hand of God, the Father Almighty?

Question 2 ◈ When did Christ ascend into heaven?

Question 3 ◈ What is meant by the redemption?

Level 5 - Lesson 6

Prayer

The Act of Faith

Having studied in some detail the Apostles' Creed, over the next few lessons we are going to examine the meaning of the Acts of Faith, Hope and Charity. These are very important prayers as they demonstrate our belief in the three theological virtues; Faith, Hope and Charity.

**O my God, I firmly believe all the truths that the
holy Catholic Church believes and teaches. I believe these truths O Lord,
because You, the infallible Truth has revealed them to her.
In this faith I am resolved to live and die.
Amen.**

We address this prayer to God, not a particular Person, but to the Blessed Trinity. When saying this prayer, we are telling God that we believe in ALL the truths of His Church. We tell Him that we believe them, not because we necessarily understand them, but that we believe them because He says so. Therefore we are telling God that whatever He teaches us, through His Church, we will believe with all our hearts and minds, because God is all Truth.

We also tell God that we intend to hold firmly to these beliefs, not just for the present, but unto death, even if we have to shed our blood to defend these truths.

When we pray the Act of Faith, let us meditate upon the sublime meaning of the words we pronounce. Each time we repeat the words of the prayer, we are affirming our faith in the Creator of the world.

Question 4 ❖ What are we telling God when we pray the Act of Faith?
Question 5 ❖ To Whom do we address the Act of Faith?
Question 6 ❖ What do we mean by life everlasting?

Bible Studies

The Conversion of Saul

Saul, still breathing threats and slaughter against the disciples of our Lord Jesus Christ, was asked by the high priest to go to Damascus, and bring the disciples who where followers of Jesus and return them back to Jerusalem as prisoners for questioning and possible execution. As he journeyed the road to Damascus, suddenly a great light from heaven shone around him. Struck as if by lightning, he fell to the ground.

At the same moment, he heard a voice saying: "Saul, why dost you persecute Me?" Saul asked: "Who are you, Lord?" The voice replied: "I am Jesus, whom you persecute." Trembling with fear, and much astonishment, Saul said: "Lord, what do you have me to do?" The Lord spoke to him: "Arise, and go into the city, and there it shall be told to you what you must do."
Saul rose up from the ground, and opened his eyes, but he had lost his sight. His companions then took him by the hand and led him into the city. There he remained three days without eating and drinking. Now, there dwelt in Damascus a disciple of Jesus, named Ananias. The Lord appeared to him in a vision, saying: "Arise, and go into the street that is called Strait, and seek, in the house of Judas, Saul of Tarsus, for behold, he prays"

Ananias answered: Lord, I have heard, from many, of this man, how great evils he has done to the saints at Jerusalem." The Lord said to him: "Go, for this man is a vessel of election to Me, to carry My name before the Gentiles, and kings, and the children of Israel. For I will show him how great things he must suffer for the sake of My name."

Ananias went, and entering into the house where Saul was, he laid his hands upon him, and said: "Saul, brother, the Lord Jesus has sent me; He who appeared to thee in the way as thou camest, that thou mayest receive thy sight, and be filled with the Holy Ghost." And suddenly there fell from the eyes of Saul, as it were scales, and he received his sight, and, rising up, was baptized. Immediately he began to preach in the synagogues that Jesus was the Son of God.

Question 7 ❖ Before Saul was struck from his horse, what was he doing in relation to the Christians?

Question 8 ❖ Saul was struck blind; who was it who cured his blindness and baptized him?

Question 9 ❖ What did Saint Philip explain to the officer of Queen Candace?

The Saints

Level 5 - Lesson 6

Saint Francis of Assisi

Two years after Saint Hugh died, a local war was being fought in Italy between the great town of Perugia and the town of Assisi, which the Perugians wanted to make their own. In the course of it a happy and wealthy young man of Assisi named Francis was taken prisoner, and, for a year, kept in captivity, in Perugia. All the time he was in prison he was longing to be free again to lead the life of pleasure to which he had become accustomed; but when at last he was set at liberty and went back to his home he found that he was discontented with all the things that he had thought he wanted. So he made preparations to go to war again, this time against the Germans, who were invading Italy.

The night before his departure he dreamt that he was in a great hall, hung with splendid armor, all marked, as the Crusaders' armor was, with a cross. "These," said a voice, "are for you and your soldiers." Francis became more excited than ever, and, as he set off, he told his friends and his family: "I know I shall be a great Prince." But he had not gone very far before he had another dream in which the same voice asked him:

"Which is better, to serve the servant or to serve the Lord?"

"Of course, to serve the Lord."

"Then why do you make the servant your master?"

Francis, realizing what this meant, left the expedition and went back to Assisi, determined to serve God, the Lord of all, in any way he could. He found that he was seeing people of his town with new eyes. Instead of the great, wealthy families who had been his friends, he noticed for the first time those who were living in terrible poverty and disease. The beggars and lepers, he realized, were not people to be passed by without looking at them, but God's children for whom Jesus Christ died. For the love of Jesus, he determined to spend the rest of his life dedicated to 'the Lady Poverty.'

He gave away all his money and possessions, even his clothes. He served the sick and the poor. And gradually he collected around him a number of other people whom he called the Friars Minor, the 'little brothers', who with him, would love people for Christ's sake, and remind them of Jesus' life and teachings.

At first there were very few of them. They lived together not far from Assisi where, around the little Chapel of Saint Mary of the Angels which the Benedictines had given them, they built huts of wattle, straw, and mud. But soon so many joined them that the Friars Minor were able to make their way all over Europe, and even to the East, to try to convert the Mohammedans.

Above all things Francis was always teaching that Christians that they must show themselves Christians by their love for one another, as Jesus had told them. His favorite festival was Christmas and it was he who was the first to have a Crib, with its 'Bambino,' in churches, to make people realize the great story of how 'Love came down at Christmas.' He even tried to persuade the Emperor to make a special law that men should provide well for birds and beasts as well as for the poor, so that every one should have a reason for rejoicing.

The animals and the birds were his friends, he called them his brothers and sisters, as well as the lovely things of nature. He composed a poem called The Canticle of the Sun, in which he praised God for Brother Sun and Sister Moon and Sister Water, so helpful and humble and pure, and Brother Fire and for all God's gifts, even Death.

The Saints

> The Canticle : *Through whom Thou givest light in the darkness*
> *And he is bright and pleasant and humble and strong*

Then, in the year 1224, almost on the very day that the first Friars Minor landed in England, God showed that He was pleased with Francis. Francis had gone with three companions far up on a mountain called Alverna, to spend forty days in prayer and fasting. As he was praying he saw an angel flying towards him with outspread wings. In the center of this vision appeared a cross. When it vanished Francis found that in his own hands and feet and side there had been printed the five wounds of Christ Himself. His longing to become like his Master had been answered.
The Feast Day of Saint Francis is October 4th.

Question 10 ❖ Why did St Francis give away all his money and possessions?
Question 11 ❖ During his forty days of prayer, what reward did God give Saint Francis?
Question 12 ❖ How was Saint Norbert converted?

Level 5 - Lesson 6

Confirmation

Dispositions for Confirmation

1) Who can be confirmed?
Anyone who has been baptized but not yet confirmed can receive this sacrament.

2) Has the Church ever confirmed infants?
Yes, in the early days of Christianity and even now in certain Eastern countries, the Church confirms infants immediately after Baptism.

3) At what age is Confirmation usually administered?
In most parts of the Church at the present day only those who have attained the use of reason are admitted to Confirmation.

4) What are the conditions required for receiving Confirmation?
1) The person must be a baptized Catholic.
2) He should be in the state of grace; that is, free from all mortal sin.
3) He should take a saint's name, one different from his baptismal name.
4) He should be well-instructed in the principal doctrines of his Faith.

5) What knowledge should a person have who is to be confirmed?
He should know the Lord's Prayer, the Angelic Salutation (Hail Mary), the Apostles' Creed, the Commandments of God, the Precepts of the Church, the doctrine of the sacraments, especially the nature and effects of the sacrament of Confirmation.

6) What should be the dispositions of the soul of the person to be confirmed?
He should make a worthy confession and spend some time in recollection so as to be prepared to receive the Holy Ghost with His sevenfold gifts.

7) Must the sacrament of Confirmation be received while fasting?
No, today candidates for Confirmation are not required to be fasting.

8) What would happen should a person present himself to receive Confirmation knowing himself to be in the state of mortal sin?
He would commit a grave sin of sacrilege and while the sacrament would be received, he would not receive its graces until he made a good confession and received absolution.

Question 13 ❖ Who can be confirmed?
Question 14 ❖ What should be the dispositions of the soul of the person to be confirmed?
Question 15 ❖ Who is the ordinary minister of Confirmation?
Question 16 ❖ Who is the extra-ordinary minister of Confirmation?

Church History

Fathers of the Church

The fourth century (300 – 400) produced many great men and Saints who played a large part in the history of the Church at that time.

Saint Basil the Great from Caesarea in Asia Minor, wrote a rule for Monks which became the common rule for all Monasteries in the East. He was made Bishop of Caesarea in 370, and with Saint Athanasius fought against Arianism.

Saint John Chrysostom, born 347, was a great preacher. He became Patriarch of Constantinople in 398 and reformed the lives of the priests. He attacked the vices of the Empress Eudoxia, and was driven into exile. He was given the name 'Chrysostom' which means 'Golden voiced'.

Saint Hillary of Poitiers, at first a pagan, became a Catholic, and in 350 the Bishop of Poitiers. He was banished to Asia Minor by Constantine because he strongly resisted the entry of Arianism into Gaul or France. He returned and was so successful in keeping Arianism out of Gaul that he was called 'The Athanasius of the West'.

Saint Ambrose was the great opponent of Arianism in Italy. He was Governor of Milan and not yet baptized, when he was chosen Bishop of Milan by the unanimous voices of the people. Saint Ambrose stood up against the Emperor Thodosius, when he ordered a massacre of the people of Thessalonica for rebellion. Ambrose excommunicated the Emperor, who eventually repented and did the penance prescribed.

Saint Jerome, born in Dalmatia, studied in Rome, became disgusted with life in Rome and went to the East to live his life at Bethlehem. Jerome lived a life of prayer and study. His great life's work was the translation of the Bible from the original Hebrew and Greek into Latin.

Pope Saint Sylvester I (314 – 355) was the first Pope to begin collecting and cataloging the Books of the Old and New Testaments of the Bible, from Gospels and letters scattered about amongst the various Catholic Churches.

From Pope Sylvester to Pope Saint Damasus (366 – 384) the Church had collected and made a complete list or 'Canon' of Holy Scriptures. This list or Canon of Scriptures was officially recognized at the General Council of Hippo in Africa in 393. The Church now placed this list or Canon together within the cover of a single book, thus giving the Bible to the world.

By the year 400 Saint Jerome had translated the Bible into Latin, the leading language of the then known world. It is called the 'vulgate' version. From Saint Jerome through the centuries, until the invention of printing, all Bibles used in Catholic Christian Churches were read by the Priests to the people. Some of the big churches chained their Bibles to pillars to prevent theft. During all these 1000 years Bibles were written by hand by the Monks in their Monasteries and then sent out to the Churches. By the year 400 we are not far away from the collapse of the Roman Empire.

Question 17 ❖ What was the great work of Saint Jerome?
Question 18 ❖ Which century produced many great men and Saints who played a large part in the history of the Church at that time.
Question 19 ❖ Which saint was chosen as a bishop before he was even baptized?
Question 20 ❖ What was the Arian heresy?

Lesson 7

Level 5

Confirmation

Catechism

The Sacraments

138. What is a sacrament?

A sacrament is an outward sign instituted by Christ to give grace.

139. How many sacraments are there?

There are seven sacraments: Baptism, Confirmation, Holy Eucharist, Penance, Extreme Unction, Holy Orders, and Matrimony.

140. Do the sacraments give sanctifying grace?

The sacraments do give sanctifying grace.

When Our Lord was on this earth, he founded a Church through which He would dispense His graces. The two main avenues of grace are the Holy Mass and the Seven Sacraments, which were all instituted by Christ Himself. To attain heaven, we must die in a state of grace; that is, we must have sanctifying grace in our souls. Thus, the importance of the Sacraments.

Question 1 ◆ What is a sacrament?
Question 2 ◆ How many sacraments are there?
Question 3 ◆ What do we mean when we say that Christ will come from thence to judge the living and the dead?

Level 5 - Lesson 7

Prayer

The Act of Hope

**O my God, relying on Thy promises,
I hope that through the Infinite merits of Jesus Christ,
Thou might grant me pardon of my sins and
the graces necessary to serve Thee in this life
and to obtain eternal happiness in the next.
Amen.**

Again, we address this prayer to the Blessed Trinity, asking that we might receive the second of the theological virtues, that of hope. We know that to attain heaven we must be free of sin, and we show great confidence in God when we hope for the forgiveness of our sins through our sorrow and amendment of our lives. The two main sins against hope are presumption (presuming that we will be saved no matter how we live our lives) and despair (believing that we are so sinful that not even God can forgive us, often leading to the taking of one's life).

Question 4 ❖ What are the two main sins against hope?
Question 5 ❖ What do we mean by the sin of presumption?
Question 6 ❖ What are we telling God when we pray the Act of Faith?

Bible Studies

Peter's Journey – He Raises Tabitha to Life

After the conversion of Saul, the Church enjoyed peace for a while throughout Judea and Samaria. Peter went about among the faithful encouraging and confirming them in the faith. During this time he performed two great miracles.

At Lydda there was a man named Eneas, who was bound to his bed for eight years, being afflicted with palsy. Peter said to him: "Eneas, the Lord Jesus Christ healeth thee. Arise, and make thy bed." Immediately he arose. Seeing this great miracle, all the inhabitants of Lydda were converted to the Lord. While Peter remained at Lydda, he was sent for in haste by some of the disciples in Joppe, not far distant, because a certain holy woman named Tabitha had just died there.

Peter, rising quickly, went to Joppe. They brought him to an upper chamber, where Tabitha lay dead. Many poor widows stood around weeping, and showed him the garments which Tabitha had made for them. Peter was touched at the sight, and, ordering all to leave the room, he knelt down and prayed. Then turning to the corpse, he said: "Tabitha, arise!" She opened her eyes, and when she saw Peter, sat up. The fame of this miracle converted very many to the Lord Jesus Christ.

Question 7 ❖ By what means did God use to convert people?
Question 8 ❖ What did Saint Peter say to Tabitha?
Question 9 ❖ Before Saul was struck from his horse, what was he doing in relation to the Christians?

Saints

Saint Albert the Great

Among the many German knights and counts who went with the Emperor to Italy on that journey, when Saint Elizabeth's husband, Ludwig, had to leave her for the first time was a very remarkable boy of about fifteen, named Albert. He was the eldest son of the Count of Bollstedt, and he was traveling to Italy in the care of his uncle, who was in the Emperor's service, in order to study at the University of Padua.

What made Albert remarkable was his interest in everything. Of all boys who have ever lived he looked most closely at what he saw. He wanted to know the 'how' and 'why' of things; and his observation was so exact that, for instance, his description of an apple from the rind to the core has never been bettered. When, as a young boy, he was learning to hunt in the woods and heaths around the family castle he would even notice and remember the behavior of wild falcons and wonder why some trees grew taller than others. When there were various kinds of fish for dinner he would examine them in detail before he started to eat them. He was the first person really to notice insects, no one studied them until four hundred years later, and he was the first to classify flowers as wing-shaped, bell-shaped, and star-shaped. The deer and the squirrels in the forest, the cattle in the fields, and the fish in the river, the spider spinning its web in a corner, all the ordinary things that most of us just notice casually, Albert would look at so carefully that he was able to give descriptions that have not been improved upon even by modern scientists with all the instruments they can now use. He was equally interested in why things happen.

When he was still in his teens at Padua he was watching some workmen cutting up blocks of marble and discussing with them why certain sculptures on them seemed out of proportion. Another day, he pushed to the front of a crowd which was watching the opening of a well and waiting anxiously to see whether a man who had been made unconscious by the vaporous gas would recover, though two of his companions had died.

When Albert grew up he wrote thirty-eight books dealing with every department of human knowledge. That was seven hundred years ago, but many of his observations on climate and botany and geography and physics might, say one of his biographers, "have been taken from a modern textbook," and in 1941 he was proclaimed the Patron Saint of all scientists.

But it was not, of course, Albert's learning that made him a saint. The reason he was interested in all natural things was because he saw in them a reflection of the wisdom of God, Who had made them. He had a passion for exact truth, because he was sure that all truth, of whatever nature, must lead to God, Who is Truth. Albert was always very careful to distinguish between what he had actually seen for himself and what other people had told him.

Before he left Italy he joined the Dominicans, and later he was sent by them to teach at the Universities of Cologne and Paris. Here his most famous pupil, whose brilliance he recognized and encouraged, was Saint Thomas Aquinas. In 1260 Albert became the head of the Dominicans in Germany and because he was ordered to, allowed himself to be made Bishop of Ratisbon. But he resigned two years later, and retired to Cologne to spend the rest of his life teaching and writing. Saint Albert had a special prayer "against temptations."

Level 5 - Lesson 7

Saints

He prayed "not to be led astray by false words about nobility, religiosity, and excessive searching after knowledge." He was himself a noble and could, if he had wished, have been one of the great rulers in Germany. He was a 'religious' and a bishop, and he knew how many people tried to look pious when they were really nothing of the kind (that is what 'religiosity' means). One of his sayings was: "It is better to give an egg for love of God when you are alive than to leave money for a cathedral full of gold when you are dead and do not need it." And, above all, this great scientist knew that there is such a thing as 'excessive' searching after knowledge, the kind of idle curiosity that just wants to know things for the sake of knowing them, or even for pride in discovering them, and not because that knowledge leads to God Who created everything.

Saint Albert's Feast Day is November 15th.

Question 10 ❖ Saint Albert was the teacher of whom?
Question 11 ❖ To which order did Saint Albert belong?
Question 12 ❖ During his forty days of prayer, what reward did God give Saint Francis?

Confirmation

The Ceremonies of Confirmation

1) How is Confirmation administered?

1) The bishop is about to confirm, with his hand extended toward those to be confirmed, prays that the Holy Ghost descends upon them with His sevenfold gifts.
2) He lays his hand upon each one, anointing him with holy chrism on the forehead by the sign of the Cross and pronouncing the sacramental words.
3) He gently strikes each one on the cheek, and finally gives all who have been confirmed his blessing.

2) Why is the forehead anointed with the sign of the Cross?

1) To teach us that sacramental grace is given in virtue of the sacrifice of the Cross only.
2) To remind those confirmed that they must not be ashamed to profess boldly their faith in Christ Jesus crucified.
3) That by this sacred unction the soul is sealed in the Holy Ghost with a spiritual, indelible mark, which enrolls those confirmed forever in the service of Christ.

3) What does the bishop say in anointing the person he confirms?

He says: "I sign thee with the sign of the Cross, and I confirm thee with the chrism of salvation, in the name of the Father, and of the Son and of the Holy Ghost."

4) What does the bishop say when he gives the blow on the cheek of those confirmed?

He says: "Peace be to you."

5) What does the blow on the cheek signify?

It reminds them that by Confirmation they were strengthened to suffer; and if necessary, even to die for Christ.

6) How should the candidates present themselves for Confirmation?

1) They should appear in decent or modest dress.
2) They should have their foreheads neat, and their hair so arranged as to leave the forehead free to be anointed.
3) They should approach the altar with due reverence and with hands joined before their chest.

Level 5 - Lesson 7

Confirmation

7) What do we hand the bishop's assistant as we kneel to receive the sacrament?

We hand him a small card which contains the name of the patron saint chosen at Confirmation; also the baptismal and family name and the name of the sponsor.

8) What should candidates do when about to be confirmed?

1) They should most fervently ask for the gifts of the Holy Ghost.
2) They should promise to live and die as loyal and faithful soldiers of Christ.
3) They should be present from the beginning of the sacred rite and remain until the bishop has given the benediction.

9) Why is a new name taken in Confirmation?

The candidate for Confirmation takes another name to the one received in Baptism to remind him:

1) That he is to place himself under the protection of another patron saint, whom he chooses as his advocate before God;

2) That he is to follow the exemplary life of the new patron, remaining steadfast until death.

10) What penance does the Bishop give to those he has confirmed?

He tells them to say the Apostles' Creed, the Our Father and the Hail Mary as penance.

Question 13 ❖ What does the bishop say in anointing the person he confirms?
Question 14 ❖ What are the two reasons a person chooses another saint's name at Confirmation?
Question 15 ❖ What should be the dispositions of the soul of the person to be confirmed?

Church History

Monks, Monasteries and Monasticism

The Monastic life had its origin in the words of Jesus Himself, "If you will be perfect, go sell all you have, give it to the poor, and follow Me". From the very beginning of Christianity there were many who did just as Jesus had said. They gave away all they had and went off to live lives of prayer and meditation, supporting themselves by their labor.

In Egypt in times of persecution, many went away to the deserts, and undisturbed by worldly cares, led lives of great holiness. At first they lived alone as hermits, but after a while many of them came together to live in monasteries, and they made one hermit the Superior.

The first Monastery was founded by Saint Anthony of Egypt. His holiness attracted many disciples. He gathered them together and made a rule of life for them to follow. One of the disciples was Saint Hilarion.

Saint Hilarion left Anthony and went and founded Monasteries in Syria and Palestine. Then before the end of the 4th Century (400) Monasteries had been set up all over the eastern Church.

Everywhere the rules followed were much the same, fasting, prayer, meditation, study and work for maintenance. Saint Basil of Caesarea finally organized the Monasteries of the eastern Church, giving them a common rule of life based on the vows of Poverty, Chastity and Obedience.

Monasticism first came into the western Catholic Church through Saint Martin of Tours. Before his death in 400, Saint Martin had founded several monasteries in Gaul. In the Monastery at Tours, Saint Patrick was with Saint Martin. But the real founder of the Monasticism in the west was Saint Benedict. In 530 Saint Benedict established the Monastery of Monte Cassino. The rule Saint Benedict gave to Monte Cassino served as a model for all future Monastic Orders.

Question 16 ❖ How did the first monastery come to be and who founded it?
Question 17 ❖ Through which saint did monasticism come into the western Catholic Church?
Question 18 ❖ Who is considered the founder of monasticism in the West?
Question 19 ❖ What was the great work of Saint Jerome?

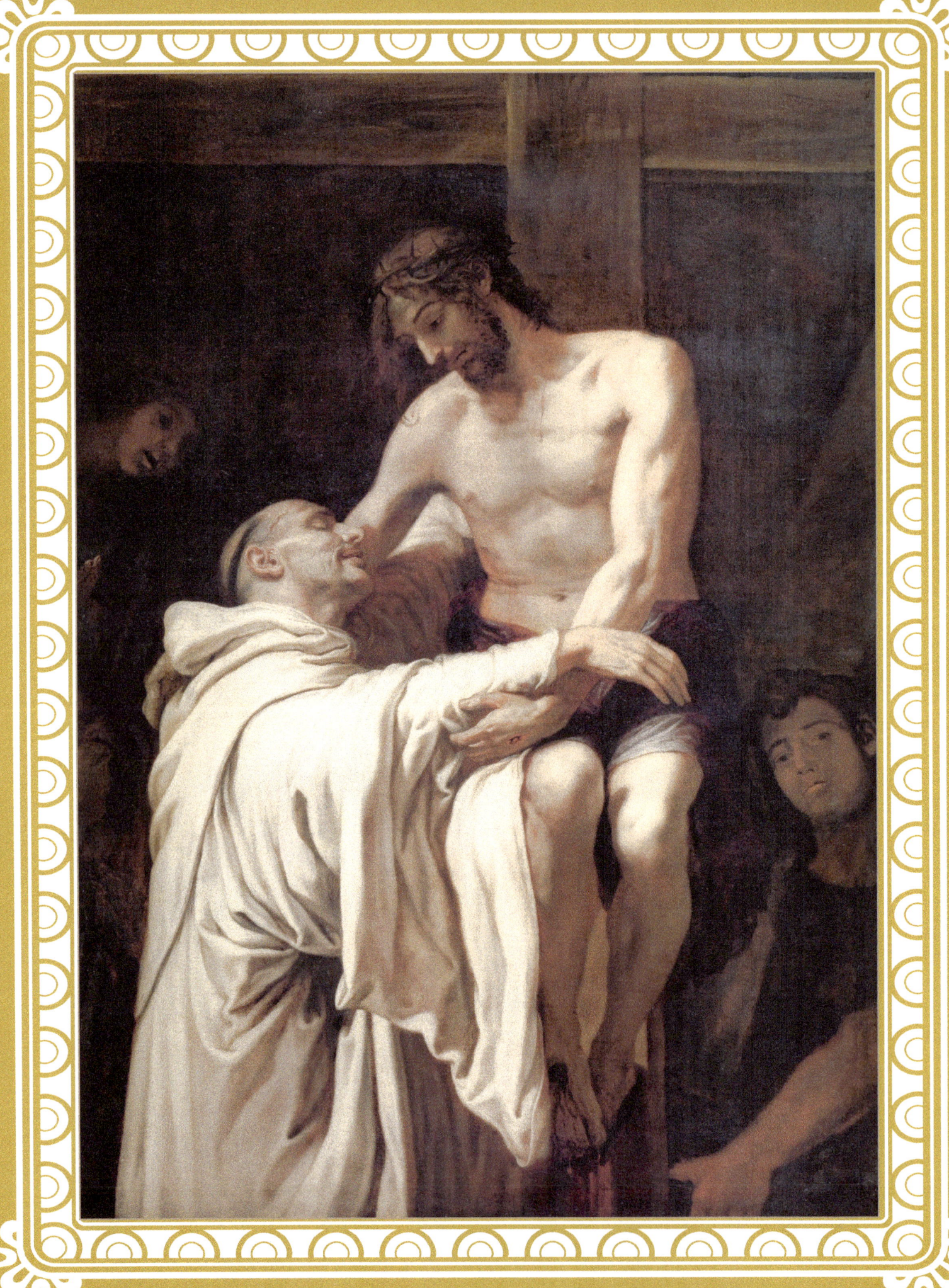

Lesson 8

Level 5

Confirmation

Catechism

The Sacraments

141. **Does each of the sacraments also give a special grace?**

    Each of the sacraments also gives a special grace, called sacramental grace.

142. **Do the sacraments always give grace?**

    The sacraments always give grace if we receive them properly.

143. **Why are Baptism and Penance called sacraments of the dead?**

    Baptism and Penance are called sacraments of the dead because their chief purpose is to give the life of grace to souls dead through sin.

As we learned in the last lesson, to attain heaven, we must die in the state of grace; that is, have sanctifying grace in our souls. It is the Sacraments (and the Mass) which are the means of achieving this end. Whenever we receive a Sacrament worthily, God floods our souls with His grace. We can be certain of this.

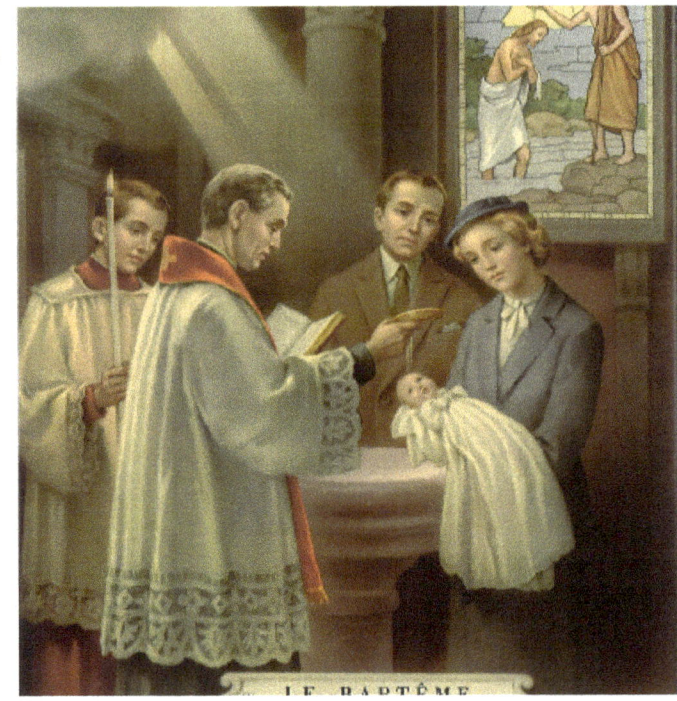

Two of the Sacraments, Baptism and Penance are referred to as Sacraments of the Dead, as they restore grace to our souls, whereas the other Sacraments add grace to a soul already in the state of grace. With Baptism, Original Sin is taken from our soul, and in its place is God's grace. The Sacrament of Penance cleans a soul of Mortal Sin, and like Baptism, replenishes the soul with God's graces.

We must strive throughout our lives to keep the grace of God in our souls; by never offending God through Mortal Sin.

Question 1 ❖ Does each of the sacraments also give a special grace?
Question 2 ❖ Why are Baptism and Penance called sacraments of the dead?
Question 3 ❖ What is a sacrament?

Level 5 - Lesson 8

Prayer

The Act of Charity

**O my God, I love Thee with all my heart
because Thou art infinitely good and perfect,
and I love my neighbor as myself for love of Thee.
Grant that I may love Thee more and more in this life
and in the next for all eternity. Amen.**

On earth, we must have faith, hope and charity. When we die and merit our eternal reward, we will no longer have need of faith, for we will see God. We will no longer have hope, for we will possess God for all eternity, but we will abide in charity forever, for we will always love God. This is why Saint Paul says that of faith, hope and charity, charity is the greatest.

Saint John the Apostle, as he was growing old nearly always gave the same short sermon. Love one another. Our Lord Himself summarized the old law (the ten commandments) into two; to love God and to love our neighbor for the love of God..

In this prayer we tell God that we love Him, that we love our neighbor for love of Him and that we will strive to love Him more each day of our lives.

Question 4 ❖ Why is charity the greatest of the theological virtues?

Question 5 ❖ Summarize the ten commandments as Our Lord did.

Question 6 ❖ What do we mean by the sin of presumption?

Bible Studies

The Conversion of Cornelius

There lived in Caesarea a man named Cornelius, a Roman centurion, a devout and God-fearing man, who gave much to the poor, and prayed continually. One day an angel appeared to him and said: "Thy prayers and thy alms have ascended for a memorial in the sight of God. Send men to Joppe, and call hither Simon, who is surnamed Peter. He shall tell thee what thou must do."

Then the angel disappeared, but Cornelius sent three men, who feared the Lord, to Joppe. On the following day as these men were drawing near the city, Peter, waiting for his midday meal, went up to the house-top to pray. During his prayer, he was rapt in ecstasy. He saw heaven opened, and behold, a great sheet, as it were, was let down by the four corners from heaven to earth.

In the sheet were all manner of four-footed beasts, and creeping things of the earth, and birds of the air. Then a voice came from heaven, saying: "Arise, Peter, kill and eat!" Peter replied: Far be it from me, Lord, for I have never eaten any common and unclean things." But the voice spoke to him again. "That which God hath purified, do not thou call common!" This was done three times, after which the vision disappeared.

Whilst Peter was wondering what this vision might signify, the Spirit of God spoke within him, saying: "Behold, three men seek you; arise, therefore, go down, and go with them, doubting nothing, for I have sent them." Immediately Peter went down and met the men whom Cornelius had sent. Next day he set out with them, and with some of his own disciples, for Caesarea. He was met by Cornelius, who, bowing down before Peter, told his vision, and all that the angel had said. Peter then understood his own vision about clean and unclean animals; that is to say, that the Gentiles, who had until now been considered unclean, were now to be received into the Church of Christ. Whereupon he announced to Cornelius and his household the doctrine of Jesus Christ.

Whilst Peter was yet speaking, the Holy Ghost came upon all who heard him. Peter and his disciples were astonished to hear these Gentiles speak in diverse tongues, even as the apostles had done on the day of Pentecost. Then Peter commanded them all to be baptized in the name of the Lord Jesus Christ. From that time on, the gospel was preached to the Gentiles in various other places. Paul, as Saul was now called, and Barnabas, his companion, preached, especially at Antioch, the ancient capital of Syria. There the number of the faithful increased very much; and there, for the first time, the believers in Christ were called Christians, after the name of the divine Founder and Master Jesus Christ.

Question 7 ❖ What did Saint Peter's ecstasy mean?
Question 8 ❖ Where were the followers of Christ first called Christians?
Question 9 ❖ What did Saint Peter say to Tabitha?

Level 5 - Lesson 8

Saints

Saint Catherine of Siena

The city of Siena is built at the top of a tall hill, and at the two highest points are the cathedral and a convent dedicated to Saint Dominic. Between them is a deep valley in which is a great well whose waters were famous all over Italy. Not far from this fountain lived in the year 1347, a dyer named Giacomo Benincasa, the youngest of whose many children was a girl name Catherine. One evening when she was about six years old she and her brother Stephen stopped to rest on the steep hill leading up to Saint Dominic's, and as Catherine was looking up at its tall tower it seemed to her that the sky suddenly opened and she saw Jesus sitting on a throne in Heaven, with Saint Peter and Saint Paul and Saint John standing beside Him. But her brother Stephen saw nothing, and he could not understand why his sister stood so still looking up into the sky. He shook her arm. She turned to him, and when she turned her eyes back again to the sky the vision had gone. She threw herself on the ground and started to cry bitterly.

From that moment she determined that she would give the whole of her life to Jesus and to no one else; and when the time came for her to marry she refused the man her father had chosen for her. Instead she asked to become a nun in the Dominican convent. But her parents would not allow this, and when Catherine still refused to marry anyone they grew angry at her disobedience. They sent away the servant and made Catherine do all the work. Her brothers and sisters made fun of her. But Catherine bore it all without complaining, for she thought, the Saints and the martyrs had to bear far worse things than this. Then one day her father found her kneeling in her room, with a white dove nestling on her shoulder. He remembered that the Holy Ghost often came in the form of a dove, and he thought that perhaps he was wrong and that it was God's will that Catherine should live as a nun, keeping herself only for Jesus, as she wished.

So Catherine became a member of the Third Order of Saint Dominic, which meant that she did not actually live in the convent but stayed at home, observing the Rule. For three years she lived in her room in absolute silence, going out only to her Communions and prayers in the great convent church on the hill-top. At the end of this time she came out of her 'desert' and went about Siena helping the sick and poor.

All the city came to love her. There was a young nobleman who had been condemned to death for a very small offence. He was very bitter about the injustice as well as being very afraid to die. Catherine went to visit him, and immediately he became calm and brave. He asked only one thing. "Stay with me!" he said to Catherine. "Then I shall be all right. I shall die content."

"Be comforted, my brother," said Catherine; "I shall be waiting for you at the place of execution."

She kept her promise. At the place of execution she was not only waiting, but she stood near him and, as she put it in one of her letters, "I bent over him and held him as he lowered his head, reminding him of the blood of Jesus."

Saints

At the time when Catherine lived the Popes had been driven out of Rome and were living in France at Avignon. They were bad times for Italy, and Catherine was quite sure that one of the reasons was the absence of the Pope. When the people of Florence, who had made the Pope very angry, asked her to go to him at Avignon and make their peace with him she set out to do so. And she did more than that. She persuaded the Pope to come back to Rome, where the Head of the Church ought to have been. After that not only the Pope but kings and rulers of republics and leaders of armies asked her advice, and she was kept so busy that several young noblemen became her secretaries and wrote the letters she dictated to them. No woman, except Saint Joan of Arc, did so much to alter the history of Europe as Saint Catherine of Siena.

But to her, of course, these things were just one of the ways she showed her love for Jesus; and the greatest day of her life was when, praying in a church before a crucifix, she found that He had given her the greatest proof of His love for her, and that on her hands and her feet and in her side were the marks of the wounds of the Crucified. Saint Catherine's Feast Day is on April 30.

Question 10   Of what Order did Saint Catherine of Siena belong?
Question 11   What happened when Saint Catherine went to Avignon?
Question 12   Saint Albert was the teacher of whom?

Confirmation

Sponsors and Parents

1) Why are sponsors taken in Confirmation?

Sponsors in Confirmation, like those in Baptism, present the candidates to the bishop and undertake to see that the child is brought up in the Catholic Faith and in the practice of his religion.

2) What is required of the sponsors in Confirmation?

1) They must be practicing Catholics.
2) They must have been confirmed and able to fulfill their duties as spiritual guardians.
3) They must be different from the baptismal sponsors.

3) How many sponsors are necessary?

There should be one sponsor for each candidate, a godfather for boys and a godmother for girls.

4) Who chooses the sponsor?

The sponsor is chosen by the candidate or by his parents or guardians; otherwise by the bishop or parish priest.

5) What are the duties of sponsors during Confirmation?

1) They should accompany the candidates and present them to the bishop at the altar.
2) While the candidate is being confirmed, they should physically touch his shoulder with their right hand, standing immediately behind him.

6) What are the duties of sponsors after Confirmation?

They should take a permanent interest in their spiritual children and should see that they receive a Christian education whenever the parents fail in this duty.

7) Does the sponsor contract a spiritual relationship?

Sponsors contract a spiritual relationship with the person for whom they stood, but this is no longer an impediment to marriage.

8) May clerics or members of religious orders act as sponsors?

No, this is forbidden without special permission.

Level 5 - Lesson 8

Confirmation

9) What are the duties of parents whose children are to be confirmed?

1) They should not neglect to have their children receive the sacrament at the proper time.
2) They must send them regularly to the preparatory instructions.
3) They should assist them in order to make a good confession before receiving Confirmation.
4) After Confirmation they must insist that their children receive the sacraments of Penance and of the Holy Eucharist frequently.

10)   What are the duties of the confirmed?

Those who have been confirmed should:

1) Thank God the Holy Ghost for the graces bestowed upon the soul.
2) Promise steadfastly to profess their Faith and live up to it.
3) Celebrate the anniversary day of Confirmation.

Question 13 ❖ What is required of the sponsors in Confirmation?
Question 14 ❖ What are the duties of sponsors after Confirmation?
Question 15 ❖ What are the two reasons a person chooses another saint's name at Confirmation?

Church History

Monks, Monasteries and Monasticism (cont)

We spoke last lesson of Saint Benedict whose rules for monasticism became a model for future monastic orders in the West from the 6th century. The Order and Rule of Saint Benedict spread rapidly through Europe. Saint Placidus took the Order to Sicily, Saint Maurus to Gaul, Saint Augustine to England. Wherever the Benedictine Monks went they took learning and culture and order and prosperity for field workers.

At times unworthy men became superiors of monasteries and then discipline and holiness declined. But from time to time saints appeared to restore full monastic fervor and life.

The Monastery of Cluny, founded in France in 909, became a house of learning and sanctity. It sent forth missionaries to all parts of Europe. Pope Saint Gregory VII came from Cluny. Other Monastic Orders appeared. In 1084 Saint Bruno started a monastery at La Chartreuse with strict rules of silence, abstinence, prayer, labor, study. In 1098 Saint Robert built the Monastery of Citeaux. In 1113 he was joined by Saint Bernard. This new Cistercian Order spread quickly. It soon had 54 Monasteries in England. In 1115 Saint Bernard founded the Monastery of Clairvaux. Bernard was one of the great figures of the Middle Ages.

During the time after the Barbarian invasions of Europe, from about 450 on to 1000, the Popes had to depend on the Monasteries for help in restoring the Catholic Faith to Europe and the Monasteries supplied many great Missionaries to the Church.

Saint Patrick, a Monk who trained with Saint Martin of Tours, was sent by Pope Celestine I to convert Ireland in 432. He became the Apostle of Ireland. Ireland became a country of sanctity and learning. It became known as the land of scholars and saints. Monasteries, Convents, Churches, schools sprang up everywhere in Ireland.

Saint Brigid, called the 'Mary of Ireland' helped Saint Patrick. Then Ireland, in her turn, sent out Missionaries to all parts of the world.

The Irish Monk Saint Columba went to Scotland. He landed on the Isle of Iona in 563 and established a Monastery there. Saint Columba and his Monks converted the Orkney Islands, the Shetlands, and even went on to Greenland and Iceland.

England had received the Catholic Faith whilst under Roman rule. After the Roman legions left England, the country was overrun by Angles, Saxons and Jutes. All were pagans. The Church was destroyed in England.

In 596 Pope Saint Gregory the Great sent the Monk Saint Augustine and forty companions to reconvert England to the Faith. Saint Augustine converted Ethelbert King of Kent. Then he converted the chief men of the Kingdom of Kent. Saint Augustine built his Cathedral at Canterbury.

Question 16 ❖ What special work did the Monasteries do from 450AD to 1000AD.?
Question 17 ❖ List three Saints who started monasteries?
Question 18 ❖ How did the first monastery come to be and who founded it?

Lesson 9

Level 5

Confirmation

Catechism

The Sacraments

144. **Why are Confirmation, Holy Eucharist, Extreme Unction, Holy Orders, and Matrimony called sacraments of the living?**

    Confirmation, Holy Eucharist, Extreme Unction, Holy Orders, and Matrimony are called sacraments of the living because their chief purpose is to give more grace to souls already alive through grace.

145. **What sin does he commit who knowingly receives a sacrament of the living in mortal sin?**

    He who knowingly receives a sacrament of the living in mortal sin commits a mortal sin of sacrilege.

146. **Why can Baptism, Confirmation, and Holy Orders be received only once?**

    Baptism, Confirmation, and Holy Orders can be received only once because they imprint on the soul a spiritual mark which lasts forever.

Last lesson we studied the two Sacraments of the Dead, Baptism and Penance. In this lesson, we learn the other five Sacraments are called Sacraments of the Living, because as the catechism question says, their purpose is to give more grace to those souls who are already in the state of grace.

The Sacraments of the living are so important and vital to our salvation, that we must be sure to receive them in the state of grace. If you are in mortal sin, you must go to Confession (Sacrament of Penance) to clean your soul and prepare to receive the other Sacraments.

Question 1 ❖ Why are Confirmation, Holy Eucharist, Extreme Unction, Holy Orders, and Matrimony called sacraments of the living?
Question 2 ❖ What sin does he commit who knowingly receives a sacrament of the living in mortal sin?
Question 3 ❖ Does each of the sacraments also give a special grace?

Level 5 - Lesson 9

Prayer

The Act of Contrition

When you were preparing for your First Confession and First Holy Communion, you learned the 'Act of Contrition'. It is a prayer that you should say every night before bed after your examination of conscience. It should also be said whenever you have sinned gravely or deliberately. Let us study this prayer in more depth over the next two lessons.

Oh my God, I am sorry and beg pardon for all my sins

We address ourselves in this prayer to our merciful God. We not only tell Him that we are sorry for the sin/s we have just committed, but for all our sins; those forgotten and those already confessed. We not only tell Him that we are sorry, but we beg Him to forgive us, because we know that if God will not forgive us, we cannot go to heaven.

I detest them above all things

We go on to say that sin is to us the greatest crime, the worst thing that we can possibly do. Yes, these words of the Act of Contrition are very powerful.

Because they deserve Thy dreadful punishments

We go on to tell God the three reasons we are sorry for our sins. The first is that we are afraid of the eternal punishment due to us should we die in the state of (mortal) sin. This is an imperfect contrition, but nevertheless, we should have a fear of God's punishment, as He is a just judge, and we know too well our guilt.

Because they have crucified my loving Saviour Jesus Christ

We know too well what suffering our sins causes the most Sacred Heart of our Divine Saviour. We think here of the Passion and Death of Our Lord. When saying this prayer, have before our eyes a crucifix or a sacred image of Our Lord upon the Cross. If we say these words with true sorrow and understanding, how can tears of sorrow not escape us?

And most of all because they offend Thy Infinite Majesty

We should be sorry, above all, because we have offended God, our Creator, our Saviour, our best Friend. This God Who is all powerful and all knowing has been offended by us, and what are we? Nothing! This is perfect contrition. We have offended the infinite Goodness by our sin and we want to tell Him that we are sorry, not for our sake, but for His.

Question 4 ◆ What is an imperfect act of contrition?
Question 5 ◆ What are the three reasons we are sorry for our sins?
Question 6 ◆ Why is charity the greatest of the theological virtues?

Bible Studies

Peter in Prison

Herod Agrippa, grandson of Herod who had caused the little children of Bethlehem to be slaughtered, was now reigning in Judea. Wishing to find favor with the Jews, he began to persecute the disciples of Jesus; and, having put James, brother of John, to death, he caused Peter to be arrested and thrown into prison.

Now, it was the time of the Jewish Passover; so Herod told the soldiers to guard Saint Peter during the festival-time, when he meant to put him to death publicly. But prayer was made unceasingly by the infant Church for Peter. Now, the night preceding the day on which he was to be put to death had already come.

That night, being bound with two chains, Peter slept between two soldiers. The other soldiers kept watch at the door of the prison. And behold, an angel of the Lord appeared to Peter, and a bright light shone all around. The angel struck Peter on the side, and awakened him, saying: "Arise, quickly!" He did so, and the chains fell from his hands.

Then the angel spoke to him: "Gird thyself and put on thy sandals, and follow me!" Peter obeyed, not knowing, however, whether it was a dream or reality. Going out, they passed through the first and the second ward, or watch, and came to the iron gate leading to the city, which opened, of itself, before them. But when they came out of the prison-yard and had passed along the street, the angel disappeared. Then Peter, coming to himself, found it was not a dream, and he exclaimed: "Now I know in very deed that the Lord hath sent His angel, and hath delivered me out of the hand of Herod, and from all the expectation of the people of the Jews!" He went then to the house of Mark, where many Christians were assembled in prayer. When Peter knocked at the door a young girl named Rhode came to listen. On hearing and recognizing Peter's voice, the girl was so delighted that she forgot to open the door, and ran in haste to tell the others. But they supposed that she had lost her mind. Yet she insisted that Peter was really at the gate. They then said that it must be his angel. Meanwhile Peter continued knocking. When the door was at length opened, and they saw it was indeed Peter, everyone was struck with amazement. Their wonder increased when they heard how the angel of the Lord had delivered him from prison. When morning came, and Peter was not to be found, the guards were filled with consternation, and well they might, for Herod hearing of Peter's escape, caused them all to be put to death. But Herod himself did not long escape the punishment which his impiety and cruelty deserved.

He had gone to Caesarea, and was seated on his throne in kingly state to receive some foreign ambassadors. He delivered an oration which drew from the people the wildest acclamation. They said he spoke as a god and not as a man. This absurd and senseless flattery was very acceptable to the tyrant. He was well pleased to be considered as a god. But immediately the angel of the Lord struck him with a terrible and loathsome disease, and he expired in fearful torments.

Question 7 ❖ Explain the miracle of Saint Peter's escape from prison.
Question 8 ❖ From the Scriptures, what was the cause of this miracle?
Question 9 ❖ What did Saint Peter's ecstasy mean?

Level 5 - Lesson 9

The Saints

Saint John of God

Saint John of God was born four years later than Saint Ignatius Loyola and died six years before him and like Ignatius, he founded a new Order in the Church: the Hospitallers or, as they are sometimes called, the Brothers of Charity. But as far as we know these two Spanish saints never met each other and certainly two men could hardly have been more different.

John was born in 1495 at Montemoro Novo in Portugal. His parents were very poor, and when he was only eight years old, John ran away from home with a traveler who had stayed for some days with them, telling tales of the wonderful things he had seen in his journeys. But the little boy found himself left alone in a village near Oropesa on the other side of Spain, four hundred and fifty miles away from home. There was no one he could turn to; it was impossible for him to get back to Montemoro, so he worked as a shepherd-boy for a farmer of the district. There John stayed till he was about twenty, serving the farmer so well that the man decided to let him marry his daughter and become a partner in the sheep-farm. But John still wanted adventure and once more he ran away – this time as a soldier of fortune in the Spanish army which was going to Hungary to fight the Turks. Until he was forty he was a trooper in various parts of Europe, enjoying the dangerous, cruel, care-free life and forgetting all about the religious duties which his mother had taught him as a small boy and which, in his days as a shepherd, he had still remembered a little.

While he was a soldier he often risked death in battle; but it was facing death in another way that brought a change in his life. After one battle he was left to guard a great heap of booty. When his turn to guard it was over and another soldier came to take his place, it was found that much of it had been stolen under his very nose. Of course everybody suspected him of partnering the thief and of getting his share of the loot; and, even if that were not true, he had certainly failed in his guard-duty. He was tried by court-martial and condemned – so one account says – to be hanged on the spot. The rope was actually round his neck when an important officer happened to pass by and, pitying him, ordered that he should be allowed to live, on condition that he immediately left the regiment.

So he returned to Spain, and at last decided to go back to his native village and his parents. When he got there he found they were both dead and he was told that his mother had been dead for many years. She had, in fact, died from grief shortly after he had run away from home, for he was her only child and she had loved him most dearly.

When John heard this, he was terribly sad and blamed himself for the deaths of his parents. He saw, too, that there were many other people to whom he had done wrong in his soldiering days and he determined to spend the rest of his life trying to make up for all the evil he had done.

Saints

His first idea was to go to Morocco and give his life in martyrdom as Ramon Lull had done, but he soon came to feel that to be chosen as a martyr was too great an honor to expect and after he had consulted a priest in Africa about it he came home to Spain. He landed at Gibraltar, where he spent what little money he had on a wheelbarrow and some religious books and pictures and statues. He trudged the roads of Spain, selling these to whoever he could, until he came to the city of Granada. While on this journey, he found a small child by the roadside, barefoot and badly clothed, just as John himself had been when he had been deserted at Oropesa. Immediately he lifted the boy on his shoulders and carried him as far as his strength would let him. When they reached a drinking-fountain, John suggested to the boy that they should stop and rest a little. The boy climbed down from his shoulders and said, holding out to him a pomegranate (which is a Pomo-de-Granada, a Granada apple): "John of God, in Granada you shall find your Cross." Then he disappeared and John did not see him again.

When John arrived in Granada, he set up a little shop by the city gates where he continued to sell books and pictures and statues, as he had done on the road. But he soon felt that this was not enough to do to serve Jesus and atone for his wicked life, so he went on a pilgrimage to Our Lady of Guadeloupe and there he was told in prayer his real life's work. When he returned to Granada, he rented another house and turned it into a home for all the outcasts of Granada. Tramps and cripples, homeless poor and prisoners just let out of jail – John gathered them all together and looked after them. When he needed money, he went out into the streets to beg for it.

Though he had hardly any education and was certainly not a doctor, he managed somehow to look after his strange 'family' as if he were doctor and nurse and priest all rolled into one. At last John's 'hospital' became so talked about in the city that the Bishop – who was also the Mayor – sent to find out who he was and why he was doing this in Granada. John told the Bishop of what the Child had said to him and of the curious name by which he had been called.

"Then," said the Bishop, "John of God shall always be your name." And he gave him help and money to carry on his work in a bigger way, with helpers and a larger 'hospital.' In this way the Order of Hospitallers was started.

One of the stories men loved to tell about John was how, when a fire broke out in his hospital, he forgot about the danger of the flames and insisted on going back again and again until all his 'family' were rescued. And it is this incident which is still remembered year by year in the prayer which is said on his feast-day, reminding us of the saint who, "burning with love of God, could walk unharmed through flames."

Saint John's Feast Day is March the 8th.

Question 10 ❖ What did Saint John do when he was eight years old?
Question 11 ❖ As an adult, Saint John regretted his actions when he was eight. What did he do to make up for these actions?
Question 12 ❖ What Order did Saint John of God found?
Question 13 ❖ What happened when Saint Catherine went to Avignon?

Level 5 - Lesson 9

Confirmation

The Seven Gifts of the Holy Ghost

What are the seven gifts of the Holy Ghost? The seven gifts of the Holy Ghost are: wisdom, understanding, counsel, fortitude, knowledge, piety, and fear of the Lord.

1) **Wisdom** is that gift by which we recognize the emptiness of earthly things. By it we come to regard God and spiritual things as of the highest good. Without the gift of wisdom we are indifferent to spiritual matters, avoiding all mortification.
2) **Understanding** is that gift by which we are enabled to recognize the true Catholic teaching, and to detect false doctrines. Before the descent of the Holy Ghost on the Apostles, they did not understand the divine mysteries Christ revealed to them, often interpreting His words materially.
3) The gift of **Counsel** helps us to discover the will of God under difficult circumstances.
4) **Fortitude** is the gift by which we are strengthened under trials, to do God's will.
5) The gift of **Knowledge** enables us to grasp the teaching of the Church, to know God and Jesus Christ whom He sent.
6) **Piety** is that gift by which we love God as our Father, ever striving to do His will.
7) The **Fear of the Lord** makes us dread sin as the greatest of all evils, and enables us to quell fear of man and human respect.

Besides these seven gifts, the Holy Ghost also grants certain extraordinary gifts, which are given only on rare occasions and to selected persons. Such extraordinary graces are granted principally not for the benefit of the recipient, but of others.

They were common during the early days of the Church, and helped in its rapid spread. Among them are the gift of tongues, of miracles, of visions, and of prophecy. The Apostles received the gift of tongues, on Pentecost, so that although they spoke to a crowd of different nationalities and languages, everybody understood what was said.

Question 14 ❖ What are the seven gifts of the Holy Ghost?
Question 15 ❖ Which gift strengthens us under trials?
Question 16 ❖ What are the duties of sponsors after Confirmation?

Church History

The Temporal Power of the Popes

Constantine the Great, left Rome in 330, and set up his Imperial Capital at Byzantium, which he renamed Constantinople. With the Emperor gone from Rome, the Pope became the most important figure in Rome. The Emperor Constantine had given to the Pope a number of palaces and a great deal of property in and around Rome. This became known as the 'Patrimony of Peter'. Its revenues were used to run the Church, and to help the poor.

Over the next 100 years (330 – 430) the power and influence of the Pope increased.
When the Western Roman Empire fell in 476, the people of Italy turned to the Pope as their chief protector. They had not forgotten how it was that Pope Leo I in 452 had saved Rome from Attila the Hun.

In 756 Pepin, the King of France, came to the help of the Pope. Pepin defeated the Lombards in battle, and the Pope was established as the ruler of Rome and the territory near the city of Rome. In 800 the Emperor Charlemagne confirmed the authority of the Pope over Rome and Papal States around Rome. These Papal States were extended to include most of central Italy. This is how the 'Temporal Power of the Popes' began, and how the Papal States were set up, with the Pope as their sovereign ruler.

As Ruler over Rome and the Papal States, the safety and independence of the Pope was guaranteed. The other Catholic Kingdoms of Europe made sure of that, and they looked to the Pope as their great leader. The Pope as the Head of the 'Catholic Church', which was an international Church, had to be independent of any one nation, in every way. As the ruler of Rome and the Papal States the Pope was truly independent.

Even when Rome and the Papal States were eventually taken from the Pope by Napoleon Bonaparte in 1805, returned, and taken away again in 1870, the final Treaty of Rome arranged by Mussolini with Pope Pius XI in 1929, had to give the Pope supreme and independent rule over a separate state called the Vatican. The Vatican is a part of Rome, but it is an independent State, and the Pope is not a subject of the Italian State.

Question 17 ❖ What was known as the 'Patrimony of Peter'?
Question 18 ❖ Who had saved Rome from Attila the Hun, and in what year?
Question 19 ❖ Why was it important that the Pope was ruler over Rome and the Papal States?
Question 20 ❖ What special work did the Monasteries do from 450AD to 1000AD.?

Lesson 10

Level 5

Confirmation

Catechism

Baptism

147. **What is Baptism?**

    Baptism is the sacrament that gives our souls the new life of grace by which we become children of God.

148. **What sin does Baptism take away?**

    Baptism takes away original sin; and also actual sins, if there be any, and all the punishment due to them.

149. **Who can administer Baptism?**

    The priest is the usual minister of Baptism, but if there is danger that someone will die without Baptism, anyone else may and should baptize.

150. **How would you give Baptism?**

    I would give Baptism by pouring ordinary water on the forehead of the person to be baptized, saying while pouring it: "I baptize thee in the name of the Father, and of the Son, and of the Holy Ghost."

The first Sacrament to be received is Baptism. No other Sacrament can be received before Baptism. It takes away the Original Sin on our souls and makes our souls clean and pleasing to God. It is also the Sacrament that makes us members of God's holy Church; the Catholic Church.

The ordinary minister of baptism is the priest, but in cases of emergency, any person (of the age of reason) can baptize, but they must use the exact words while the water is running over the forehead of the person being baptized.

Baptism is usually given to babies as soon as possible after they are born. Some parents put off this important duty which is both dangerous and sinful. Think of the consequences if a parent did not baptize the baby and the baby died; it could not go to heaven.

Question 1 ❖ What sin does Baptism take away?
Question 2 ❖ How would you give Baptism?
Question 3 ❖ Why are Confirmation, Holy Eucharist, Extreme Unction, Holy Orders, and Matrimony called sacraments of the living?

Level 5 - Lesson 10

Prayer

The Act of Contrition (continued)

I firmly resolve by the help of Thy grace never to offend Thee again

After telling God that we are sorry for having offended Him, we make the next important step in true contrition. We tell God, that by means of His grace and our will, we intend never to offend Him again. This is very important. If we stole from someone a large amount of money and then said sorry, but had every intention of stealing again, it shows our sorrow was never sincere. When we confess, we must have the intention of not doing it again.

And carefully to avoid the occasions of sin.

We must not only have the intention of not sinning again, but we must take the necessary means to avoid the occasion of that sin. For example, an alcoholic who is sorry for getting drunk, but he still persists in walking past the hotel every night, knowing that the temptation is often too much for him, and consequently, he finds himself drinking again and again -this is not avoiding the occasion of sin.

Amen

So be it. I agree.

Question 4 ❖ Why must we resolve not to sin again?

Question 5 ❖ Why must we resolve to avoid the occasions of sin?

Question 6 ❖ What is an imperfect act of contrition?

Bible Studies

Saint Paul's First Mission (AD 45 to 48)

The Holy Ghost commanded the chief men of the Christians of Antioch to set apart Paul and Barnabas for the work to which they were called. Then after they had prayed and fasted, they imposed hands upon both of them, and sent them forth to preach the gospel. Then it was that Paul began in all earnest to labor for the conversion of the pagan world.

He preached first to the Jews. But they still refusing to receive the divine gift of faith, he took himself to the Gentiles. Many of these heard with delight the word of life, and were baptized, so that the Church of Jesus Christ increased from day to day. Then Paul and Barnabas went to Cyprus, the native country of Barnabas. After they had preached throughout the whole island, the pro-consul, Sergius Paulus, sent for them, that he might hear from their mouth the word of God.

There was with Sergius a Jew, a false prophet named Bar-Jesus. This man resisted them to his utmost, and endeavored to dissuade Sergius from becoming a Christian. But Paul, full of the Holy Ghost, looked on him, and said: "O thou, full of all guile and of all deceit, son of the devil, enemy of all justice; thou dost not cease to pervert the right ways of the Lord. And now behold, the hand of the Lord is upon thee, and thou shall be blind, not seeing the sun for a time!"

Immediately a thick mist came before his eyes, and he went about groping for some one to take him by the hand. The pro-consul, seeing this miracle, believed in the Lord Jesus Christ. From Cyprus, Paul and Barnabas sailed for Asia Minor. Having come to Antioch, in Pisidia, they entered into the synagogue on the Sabbath-day, and preached to the people of Jesus crucified and risen again from the dead, with the remission of sins through Him alone.

Paul's discourses pleased the people so much that he was requested to come on the following Sabbath and preach again. But the Jews were filled with envy, seeing the multitude that came on that second Sabbath to hear Paul, and they contradicted all he said. Then Paul and Barnabas spoke boldly: "To you it behooved us to speak first the word of God; but seeing that you reject it, and judge yourselves unworthy of eternal life, behold, we turn to the Gentiles."

The Gentiles, hearing this, rejoiced, and the gospel was proclaimed throughout the whole land. The Jews, however, incited a persecution against Paul and Barnabas, and they were expelled from that country. The two apostles, shaking the dust from their feet, went to Iconium, where Paul preached the gospel.

Among those who heard him was a man who had been a cripple from his birth, and had never walked. Paul, looking at him, perceived that he had the faith, and said with a loud voice: "Stand upright on thy feet!" The cripple leaped up and walked. The multitude, seeing this, cried out: "The gods, in the likeness of men, are coming down to us!" And they called Barnabas, on account of his height, Jupiter; and Paul they called Mercury, because of his eloquence.

Even the priest of Jupiter, bringing oxen, with garlands of flowers, to the gate, would have offered sacrifice with the people, to Paul and Barnabas. But they, seeing what was going on, rent their

Bible Studies

garments, and ran among the people crying out: "O men, why do ye these things? We also are mortals, men like unto you, preaching to you to be converted from these vain things to the living God, who made heaven and earth and the sea, and all things that are in them. Who, in past generations, suffered all nations to walk in their own way. Nevertheless, He left not Himself without testimony, doing good from heaven, giving rains and fruitful seasons, filling our hearts with food and gladness." Hearing this, many believed in the word of God. But some Jews, who had come from Antioch and Iconium, stirred up the people against Paul. They stoned him until they thought he was dead, and cast him out of the city.

But while the disciples of the city, who had gone out, stood weeping around him, he rose up and departed to Derbe and then returned to the cities where they had already preached. They exhorted the disciples to persevere, ordained priests for them in every church, and, with fasting and prayer, commended them to the Lord. Finally, they returned to Antioch and told of the great things which God had done to them, and through them, and how He had opened the door of faith to the Gentiles.

Question 7 ❖ To whom did Saint Paul principally preach?
Question 8 ❖ Who went preaching with Saint Paul in those early years?
Question 9 ❖ How did the Jews react towards Saint Paul?
Question 10 ❖ Explain the miracle of Saint Peter's escape from prison.

Saints

Saint Camillus De Lellis

Camillus was born near Naples in 1550, the year in which, in Spain, Saint John of God died. He was the son of a wild father who cared only for fighting and gambling and was usually away at the wars. Camillus' mother died when he was twelve, and the boy was taken charge of by relatives. They could do little with him. He was lazy and disobedient; he had a violent temper and always wanted his own way; and out of school hours he spent his time with bad companions. So his relatives were glad to be rid of him when at sixteen a lanky figure, already over six foot, he went off to join his father in camp and become a soldier.

The chief thing his father taught him was to be an expert gambler, and the two of them, when they were not fighting for some captain or other (for they sold their services to anyone who would pay them), used to tramp about Italy, winning money from whoever was foolish enough to play cards with them. But before very long the father became ill and died, very sorry for the way he had lived, and Camillus, who had nursed him and was now left alone in the world, decided that he too must try to lead a different kind of life. He went off to find one of his uncles who was a Franciscan, hoping to be allowed to become a friar. But, as he had become lame from a wound in his ankle which would not heal, this was impossible. When that was better, they said, and he was fit for the hard life they led, he might come back.

So Camillus went to hospital, and, as he had no money, he offered to pay for the treatment by becoming a servant there. All went well until he taught the other servants to gamble. Then they started to quarrel and neglect their work and those in charge of the hospital, when they discovered a pack of playing-cards hidden in Camillus' bed, sent him away there and then, with his ankle still unhealed and without any money in his pocket. He went back to soldiering and his old life. For the next five years he fought, first by land and sea, for Venice against the Turks, then for Spain in North Africa, defending Tunis, and finally for a company of adventurers whom he asked to join, because every man in it was said to be a gambler. At last, at the age of twenty-five, he realized that, what with the wild life he had led and his bad foot, his days of soldiering were over. When the company was disbanded he returned to Naples, where he immediately gambled away all that he possessed – his gun, his sword, his powder-flasks, even his coat.

With nothing left but his shirt, he turned beggar. One day when he was standing outside a church asking for alms a man went up to him and told him that such a one as he, young and strong in spite of his lameness, should be working for his living, not standing there begging. Camillus said that he was a disbanded soldier and that no one would employ him. The man immediately offered him a job as a bricklayer on a new monastery which was being built. Camillus, in spite of the laughter of his companion and of his own fear that after his exciting life he would never be able to endure the dullness of such an occupation, took it.

At first, of course, it was not easy for him, nor did he all at once give up his old habits. But he persevered until he had so far got the better of them that he decided to go back to the hospital which had once turned him out. And this time there were no complaints. He stayed there for five years, helping to nurse the sick, and some one who saw him wrote, "I know not what more the most loving mother could have done for her sick child." He determined to go one step further and become a priest, and so he, who had been so lazy and rebellious in his schooldays, went back to school at the age of thirty-two and sat quietly among small boys, who nicknamed him "the Late Arrival," learning Latin grammar.

Camillus' ambition was now to serve the poor and the outcasts whom no one else cared for. Because of his early life, he understood them and knew how terrible for them sickness could be. So he gathered round him others who thought as he did, and they made a vow that wherever there was pain and illness and death, no matter how dangerous the place, they would go to the rescue. On their shoulders they wore a Red Cross of the Crusaders, and with this as their badge they went into vile dens, where people were dying of the plague,

Level 5 - Lesson 10

Saints

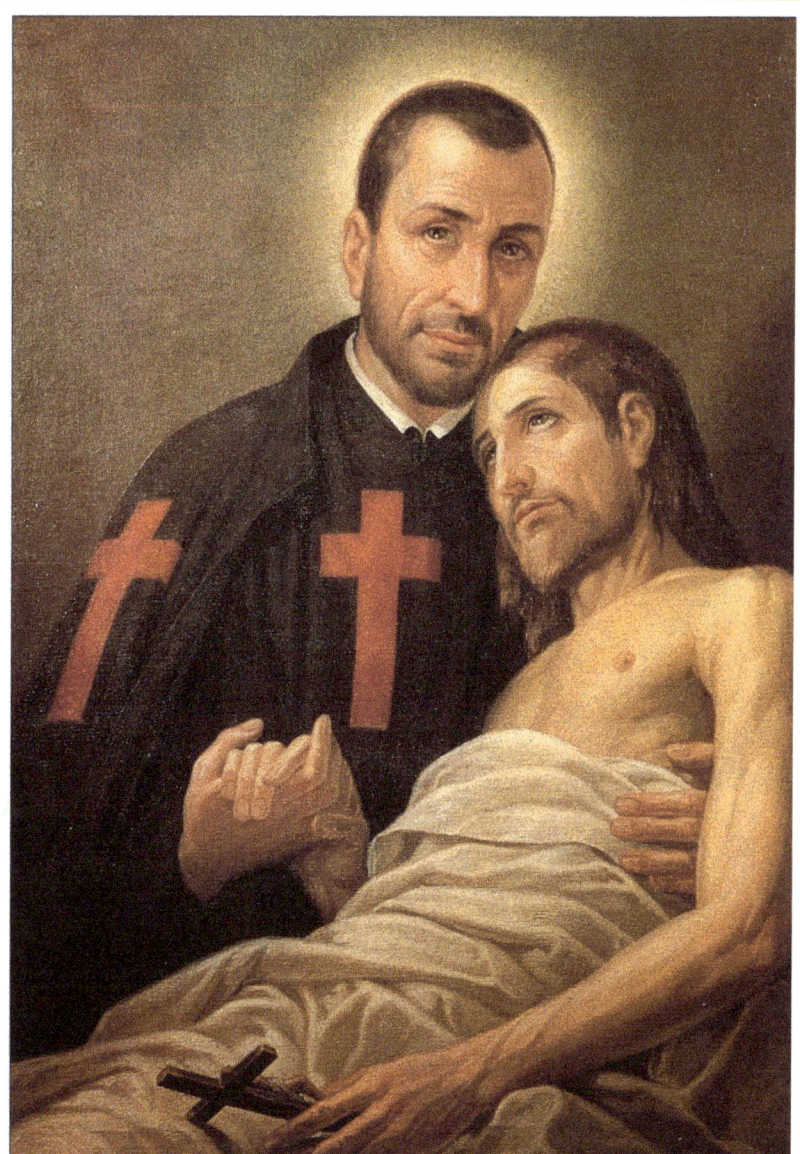

in prisons, where men were condemned to death, on to battlefields, among convicts in the galleys. Camillus' Congregation of Nursing Brothers or, as they were sometimes called, the Brothers of a Happy Death, was the original Red Cross movement. To Camillus, the one-time soldier, we owe the first field ambulances and advanced dressing-stations and field hospitals. But Camillus, the one time down and out gambler, tried equally to help those who were what he once had been.
He still gambled, though in a different way. He took risks about people's goodness that no one else would take. Once, when he gave clothes to some ragged beggars, they immediately sold them and then started to run away before Camillus should see what they had done. But Camillus brought them back, and without a word gave them some more clothes. When people told him that this was going too far and that such men were beyond help, he said, "What, my brothers, do you see nothing but the rags of these poor creatures? And do you see nothing beneath the rags but the poor creatures themselves?" He then reminded them of Jesus' saying, "In as much as you have done it unto one of the least of these my brethren, you have done it unto me." To the end Camillus served the outcast and the dying wherever they might be, because, in so doing, he was serving Christ Himself. When he could hardly move from the pain in his foot and was so ill that everything he ate made him sick he still managed to visit the beds of the dying and give them what help and comfort he could. When he himself came to die he lay with them in a common infirmary. After asking men to pray for him, "a great sinner, a gambler and a man of bad life," the Saint stretched out his arms in the form of a cross, murmured the words, "Most Precious Blood," and died "without a shudder or a change of his countenance."
The Feast Day of Saint Camillus De Lellis is July 18th.

Question 11 ❖ What was the first turning point in Saint Camillus' life?
Question 12 ❖ What was Saint Camillus' nursing brothers sometimes called?
Question 13 ❖ As an adult, Saint John of God regretted his actions when he was eight. What did he do to make up for these actions?

Confirmation

The Seven Gifts of the Holy Ghost (continued)

How do the gifts of the Holy Ghost help us?

The gifts of the Holy Ghost help us by making us more alert to discern and more ready to do the will of God.

> 1) If we look with discerning eyes, we can see how the gifts of the Holy Ghost have greatly helped the world at large.
>
> 2) The operations of the Holy Ghost were easily discernible among the early Christians.
>
> 3) The difference between the virtues and the gifts of the Holy Ghost consists in this: the virtues enables us to do what our reason directs; the gifts make us follow the inspirations of the Holy Ghost.

Which are some of the effects in us of the gifts of the Holy Ghost?

Some of the effects in us of the gifts of the Holy Ghost are the fruits of the Holy Ghost and the beatitudes. We will study the fruits of the Holy Ghost in the next lesson.

Question 14 ◆ What are two effects in us of the gifts of the Holy Ghost?

Question 15 ◆ What is the difference between the virtues and gifts of the Holy Ghost

Question 16 ◆ What are the seven gifts of the Holy Ghost?

Church History

Mohammedanism

The Church had survived three centuries of persecution, dealt with the great heresies of Arius (318), Nestorius (430) and Pelagius (400), had survived the fall of the Roman Empire, and had met the challenge of the invading hordes of Barbarians, Huns, Vandals, Goths, Lombards, Franks, Angles and Saxons. But from 650 onwards still another great enemy of the Church began to build up, an enemy which first destroyed the Church in the East in Asia, and then became a very dangerous threat to the Church in the West in Europe. This great new enemy – Mohammedanism.

It was a new religion, founded by Mahomet or Mohammed, an Arabian. He claimed revelations from God which he wrote into his book, the Koran. In 622 his own tribe expelled him from Mecca, a town half way down along the Red Sea in Arabia. He went to Medina, a town north of Mecca.

Mohammed gathered some followers in Medina, and set out on what well might have become world conquest for Mohammedanism. The Mohammedan religion was spread more by force of arms than by true religious conviction, but once converted Mohammedans remained very loyal to their religion. Mohammed first captured Mecca, and soon had all Arabia under his control. His successors continued his conquests and by 650 Syria, Palestine, Egypt and Persia had fallen to Islam, as the new religion was called.

In 707 North Africa fell into Islam. In 708 Islam forces crossed the Gibraltar straits into Spain, and occupied most of Spain. They were never able to subdue Aragon in the far north west of Spain. They swept on across the Pyrenees into France, and by 730 they had conquered nearly half of France. They even got into Sicily and became a threat to Rome.

In 732 the Mohammedan or Islamic forces were stopped and soundly defeated by Charles Martel, King of France, at the battle of Tours. The battle of Tours was one of the decisive battles in history. It turned the tide against Moslem invasions of Europe. They were never again the same threat to Europe. The Moslems, however, were not dislodged from Spain for another seven centuries.

As the Christian Kingdoms of Spain grew in power, they pushed the Moslems back into Africa. It was not until 1492 that Ferdinand and Isabella of Aragon-Castille finally drove Mohammedan power out of Spain. Then began for Spain her greatest century. In 1492 Columbus discovered the new world, and opened up to Spain the riches of the new world.

Back in the East, Islam spread through Mesopotamia, Persia, India and into central Asia. From Syria it went into Asia Minor. The Eastern Emperors at Constantinople were weak and did not oppose the Islam invaders. By the 10th Century (1000) all Asia Minor was under Moslem rule. The Church and all her institutions in Antioch, Ephesus and Smyrna, were completely destroyed.

Question 17 ◆ What has been the great enemy of the Church since 650AD?
Question 18 ◆ How was the religion of Islam spread?
Question 19 ◆ What battle turned back the Moslem invasions on Europe and in what year?

Lesson 11

Level 5

Confirmation

Catechism

Confirmation

151. What is Confirmation?

Confirmation is the sacrament through which the Holy Ghost comes to us in a special way and enables us to profess our faith as strong and perfect Christians and soldiers of Jesus Christ.

152. Who is the usual minister of Confirmation?

The bishop is the usual minister of Confirmation.

153. Why should all Catholics be confirmed?

All Catholics should be confirmed in order to be strengthened against the dangers to salvation and to be prepared better to defend their Catholic faith.

The Sacrament of Baptism leaves an indelible (permanent) mark on our souls. It can only ever be received once. The Sacrament of Confirmation is the same. The Holy Ghost comes to us in this Sacrament in a special way, to 'confirm' us in our baptismal promises, that we may be made adult Catholics, soldiers of Christ. A child usually receives this Sacrament at about the age of ten. The indelible mark of Confirmation which is impressed upon our souls, gives us a special place in heaven should we merit such a reward from God for our lives.

Question 1 ❖ What is Confirmation?
Question 2 ❖ Why should all Catholics be confirmed?
Question 3 ❖ What sin does Baptism take away?

Level 5 - Lesson 11

Prayer

The Confiteor

The Confiteor is said at every Mass, at the prayers at the foot of the Altar and before Communion. It is a public confession of our sins; not individually, but the fact that we are sinners.
We will study this prayer over the next two lessons.

**I confess to Almighty God, to Blessed Mary, ever Virgin,
to Blessed Michael the Archangel, to Blessed John the Baptist,
to the Holy Apostles Peter and Paul,
to all the saints, and to you, Father,**

This 'confession' we are making is indeed a public confession. We are not only confessing to God, but to the whole heavenly court, from Mary to the least of the saints. Additionally, we are confessing to the priest. This prayer is therefore an act of humility.

That I have sinned exceedingly in thought, word and deed.

What are we confessing to the heavenly court? Simply that we are sinners, but not only sinners by our actions and words, but even our secret thoughts.

Question 4 ❖ To whom do we address the Confiteor?
Question 5 ❖ When is the Confiteor usually prayed?
Question 6 ❖ Why must we resolve not to sin again?

Bible Studies

The Council of Jerusalem (AD 51)

Some disciples, who were formerly Jews, came to Antioch, and said to the Christians there: "Unless you be circumcised after the manner of Moses, you cannot be saved." Paul and Barnabas opposed this doctrine. But, in order to settle the question, they went up to Jerusalem to consult with Peter and the other apostles.

When Paul and Barnabas arrived in Jerusalem, the apostles and the priests assembled in council to consider the matter. After much discussion, Peter rose up and said: "Men, brethren, you know that in former days God made choice among us, that the Gentiles, by my mouth, should hear the word of the gospel, and believe.

"And God, who knoweth the hearts, gave them testimony, giving to them the Holy Ghost as well as to us, and made no difference between us and them, purifying their hearts by faith. Now, therefore, why tempt you God to put a yoke upon the necks of the disciples, which neither our fathers nor we were able to bear. But by the grace of the Lord Jesus Christ, we believe to be saved, even as they."

James, bishop of Jerusalem, spoke to the same effect. It was then decreed by the whole council of Jerusalem that the Christians at Antioch, or elsewhere, were no longer bound to observe the law of Moses. This decree commenced with these remarkable words: "It hath seemed good to the Holy Ghost and to us to lay no further burden upon you." We see that even in the first council, in which the apostles were assembled, the word and voice of Peter finished the doubt and the dispute. But as the doctrine of Peter was infallible, so the teaching of his successors in Rome is also infallible.

Question 7 ♦ What was decided at the Council of Jerusalem?
Question 8 ♦ In what year was the Council of Jerusalem?
Question 9 ♦ How did the Jews react towards Saint Paul?

Level 5 - Lesson 11

The Saints

Saint Vincent De Paul

In the year 1576, when Blessed Edmund Campion was teaching at Prague and Saint Teresa was still founding new convents in Spain, a boy named Vincent was born to a farmer in Pouy, a village in the south west of France. Like Saint Joan, Vincent, when he was small, looked after his father's sheep; but his parents were quite sure he would never be a farmer, and though they were very poor, they managed to save enough money to send him to school. He studied hard and at last was able to go to a university in Spain, where he passed all his examinations and became a priest.

As he was coming back to France by sea the ship he was in was captured by Turkish pirates, and taken to Tunis in Africa; and Vincent, who was twenty-five, found himself in the slave-market, being sold as a slave. He was bought by a fisherman, who sold him to an old alchemist, and finally he belonged to a Frenchman who lived in Africa and had turned Mohammedan. Vincent converted his last master back to the Faith; and together they escaped and managed to get back to France, where after more travels including a visit to Rome, Vincent became the parish priest of a little place not far from Paris called Clichy. But he did not stay there long. An important French nobleman, Gondi, sent for him to become tutor to his children. The two men became lifelong friends.

Gondi was the General of the Galleys, that is to say he was responsible for seeing that the king's ships were properly manned. In those days the galleys were rowed by convicts chained to their oars and continually whipped like animals when they showed signs of being tired. When they were not at sea they were crowded into damp dungeons with chains on their legs and given for their food only water and black bread.
Vincent persuaded Gondi to appoint him Chaplain to the Galleys, and immediately when he got this position he set to work to bring hope into the lives of these hopeless men. He had known what it was to be a slave and, because of that, he was perhaps the only person in the whole of France who could have helped them. One day, when he was with Gondi visiting the fleet, one of the galley slaves fainted at the oar. Vincent quietly took his place. The convicts learned to love and trust him. He served them in any way he could, doing what was possible to lessen their sufferings; and at last, by asking for money from the wealthy people that he met in Gondi's palace, he built a hospital for them.

But there were others besides galley convicts who were poor and outcast and miserable. In Paris alone, four out of every fifty people had absolutely nothing they could call their own and only managed to keep alive by begging and looking for scraps to eat. There were thousands of children, whom their parents did not want, in institutions where they were ill treated or died of hunger, or even worse, made lame or blind or in some way deformed so that they could be used as sideshows in fairs or hired out to people who made them beg on the roadside. Then there were the country laborers, who kept working like cattle so that they seemed like "black animals." But above all, for Vincent who never forgot these, there were the Christian slaves in Africa, at least forty thousand of

Saints

them, including many French and English boys.

Vincent wanted to help them all and he set about it in a very sensible way. He knew that the rich people he met were not really as selfish as they seemed. They just had not thought about the way they were treating the poor. Many of them were not as happy as they seemed either. The Court life, which seemed so happy and splendid, was often very dull and always very empty. So Vincent went to them and pleaded the cause of the poor and the outcast and especially of the children of the slaves. No one in France's history had thought of doing this before in the way that Vincent did it. He asked the rich and the well born for money and what was more difficult, service. He got both. He got enough money to build hospitals, ransom slaves and train priests who would go into the countryside.

At first these priests lived together in a monastery dedicated to Saint Lazarus, the poor man who sat at the rich man's gate in the parable that Jesus had told. They were called Lazarists, and the part of Paris where they lived is still commemorated in the name of the railway station which now stands there – Saint Lazare. Vincent sent his Lazarists not only over all France but abroad to Ireland, up to the Scottish Hebrides, to Egypt and Brazil and Madagascar and China.

But the most extraordinary thing he did was to persuade many wealthy and famous women to give up their lives in the fashionable world and to visit and help the sick and poor. He called them his Sisters of Charity, and so many people joined them that they grew into a great order and the wide white hats that Vincent made their "uniform" are still worn by those who do the same work now, four hundred years later.

It is not surprising that when the King of France, Louis XIII, knew that he was dying he sent for Vincent, so that he might die in his arms. "O, Monsieur Vincent," he said, "if I am restored to health I shall appoint no bishops unless they have spent three years with you." And after his death Vincent was always asked who he thought should be made a bishop, so that the whole church in France might show the charity of Christ which had been so forgotten.

Vincent was over eighty when he himself died. He had become so feeble that he could only raise himself from his bed by a cord nailed to a hook in the ceiling. But he never stopped organizing his charities and seeing that all the money that now came to him was used as best it could be. He knew that his followers would see that the work went on.

"Ready," he used to whisper, thinking that death had come for him. And when at last it did come one September morning at four o'clock – the time when he always got up to pray – he said, "I believe," then, "I trust," and did not speak again.

The Feast of Saint Vincent de Paul is July 19th.

Question 10 ❖ What type of people did Saint Vincent spend his life helping?
Question 11 ❖ What was the name of the Religious Order of nuns started by Saint Vincent
Question 12 ❖ What was Saint Camillus' nursing brothers sometimes called?

Confirmation

Confirmation

The Twelve Fruits of the Holy Ghost

If we co-operate with grace and use the theological virtues of faith, hope, and charity, and the cardinal virtues of prudence, justice, temperance, and fortitude, we perform good acts. These acts are called fruits of the Holy Ghost. There are twelve:

Charity : loving God and our neighbor;

Joy : having interior happiness;

Peace : living at rest with God and man;

Patience : bearing sorrows and troubles for God;

Goodness : doing good wherever and whenever we can;

Long suffering : being patient with our own faults and imperfections and also those of our neighbor;

Mildness : bearing quietly the troubles caused by others;

Faith (fidelity) : keeping our promises;

Benignity : feeling kindly toward our neighbor;

Modesty : being pure in outward appearance and manner;

Continency : preserving purity in thoughts, words, and actions;

Chastity : keeping our mind and body in that purity which our state of life demands.

Question 13   What are the three theological virtues?
Question 14   What are the four cardinal virtues?
Question 15   How do we acquire the fruits of the Holy Ghost?
Question 16   List the Twelve fruits of the Holy Ghost

Church History

The Great Schism in the East

When Pope Sylvester III crowned Charlemagne as the Emperor of the Holy Roman Empire in 800, it meant a complete break with the Eastern Empire based in Constantinople. The anger and hostility aroused in the Eastern Bishops because of this even came to a head with Pope Nicholas the Great in 858.

The Patriarch of Constantinople had become largely dependent on, and subject to, the Emperor. When the rightful Patriarch, Ignatius, rebuked the Emperor, Michael III, for immorality, the Emperor appointed Photius as the Patriarch instead of Ignatius.

Photius tried, by persecuting Ignatius, to get him to resign, then he defied a ruling of Pope Nicholas, and in 867 went into open schism with Rome. He even called a Synod of Eastern Bishops, where he excommunicated Pope Nicholas, and accused him of heresy. Photius declared that Rome had corrupted the Faith by adding the word 'Filioque' to the Creed, which means that the Holy Spirit proceeds from the Father and the Son in the Blessed Trinity.

Pope Adrian II deposed and excommunicated Photius, and reinstated Ignatius. At the death of Ignatius, Photius again took over and in spite of repeated excommunications, clung to the Patriarchal office until his death in 886. Peace followed between East and West until about 1050, when the Photian Schism was again renewed by the Patriarch of Constantinople, Michael Cerularius. This Schism went on from there, ever widening, and all efforts at reunion have since failed.

Feudalism

Whilst the great Eastern Greek Schism was in the making, the political and social system called Feudalism, was spreading everywhere through Christendom.

It was a necessity of the times, and was developed for mutual protection. Governments in those turbulent days were unable to protect the weak. The Lords and Barons had large estates from their Kings. Small land owners and peasants turned for help to these Lords and Barons. Their castles were fortified, and in return for protection the farmers and peasants worked the estates of the Lords and Barons. In time great numbers of self-contained, self-governing groups appeared.

This feudal System was to become a grave danger to the spiritual liberty of the Church. The Kings and Princes of Europe, in gratitude to the Church for her work in the dark ages of the fall of the Roman Empire, and the Barbarian invasions, had given much land and property to the Monasteries and Bishops.

Now to protect and defend herself, the Church had to turn to the secular powers. The more she did this, the more did the Church come under the control of Kings and Princes of the world. The Feudal System was to lead to great disasters and sufferings for the Church in future ages.

Question 17 ❖ In what year did the east go into open schism with Rome?
Question 18 ❖ Explain what is meant by the Feudal System?

The Four Evangelists

Lesson 12

Level 5

Confirmation

Catechism

The Holy Eucharist

154. What is the Holy Eucharist?

The Holy Eucharist is a sacrament and a sacrifice. In the Holy Eucharist, under the appearances of bread and wine, the Lord Christ is contained, offered, and received.

155. When did Christ institute the Holy Eucharist?

Christ instituted the Holy Eucharist at the Last Supper, the night before He died.

156. What happened at the Last Supper when Our Lord said: "This is My body … this is My blood"?

When Our Lord said, "This is My body," the bread was changed into His body; and when He said, "This is My blood," the wine was changed into His blood.

Saint Padre Pio once said that the Earth could more easily exist without the sun than without the Holy Sacrifice of the Mass. He was not joking! We sometimes forget the importance of the supernatural life. We might spend hours exercising, dieting and making our bodies comfortable so that we might live a longer and more healthy life, but do we spend time in looking after our eternal soul; time in preparing for heaven? What better way can we prepare for heaven than by the participation at Mass and the reception of the Blessed Sacrament (Holy Eucharist).

We cannot fully understand the miracle of the Holy Eucharist; how bread and wine, without changing their appearance, are changed into the Body, Blood, Soul and Divinity of Jesus Christ. It does not matter if we cannot fully understand it (priests spend many years studying it in the Seminary), but we believe it by Faith. Learn these questions well, they are very important. If we realize what the Holy Eucharist is, we would treat It with much more reverence, as did some of the saints who would walk on their knees to receive Our Lord.

Question 1 ❖ When did Christ institute the Holy Eucharist?
Question 2 ❖ What is the Holy Eucharist?
Question 3 ❖ What is Confirmation?

Level 5 - Lesson 12

Prayer

The Confiteor (continued)

Through my fault, through my fault, through my most grievous fault

Not once, not twice, but three times we accuse ourselves of being sinners, stating that the sins we commit are our fault. So many people like to blame others for their sins and faults, but in this prayer we state clearly that we know that we are the cause of our own sins.

**Therefore I beseech blessed Mary ever Virgin,
blessed Michael the archangel,
blessed John the Baptist,
the holy apostles Peter and Paul,
all the Saints, and you, Father,
to pray to the Lord our God for me.**

In the second half of this prayer, we pray to the heavenly court a second time; this time, not confessing our sins, but imploring their intercession before God, because we realize the gravity and number of our sins.

Question 4 ❖ What is the difference between the first and second time we pray to the heavenly court?
Question 5 ❖ Why do we say, 'Through my fault, through my fault, through my most grievous fault'?
Question 6 ❖ When is the Confiteor usually prayed?

Level 5 - Lesson 12

Bible Studies

The Second Mission of Saint Paul (AD 51 to 54)

Some time after, Saint Paul set out on another apostolic journey. He preached with great zeal in Syria, Cilicia, Phrygia, Lycaonia, Galatia, Mysia, and nearly all Asia Minor. At last he came to Troas. There he doubted where he should go next: but God made it known to him in a vision. During the night he saw, as it were, a man of Macedonia, who said to him: "Pass over into Macedonia and help us!"

Immediately, Paul set out for Europe, with his companions Silas, Luke, and Timothy, and landed safely in Philippi, the capital of Macedonia. On the Sabbath day Paul preached the Gospel of Christ. Among his hearers was a God fearing woman named Lydia, a seller of purple. Opening her ears and her heart to the divine word, she received it with joy, and was baptized with her whole family.

Very soon, however, a storm was raised against the place of prayer, they were met by a certain girl, who had a spirit of divination, and was, therefore, a source of great gain to her masters. She persisted in following the apostles crying out: "These men are servants of the Most High God, who show to you the way of salvation!"

Paul, turning round, said to the spirit that possessed her: "I command thee, in the name of Jesus Christ, to go out of her." And the spirit left her. Then her masters, seeing that the hope of their gain was gone, seized Paul and Silas, and brought them into the market place before the magistrates, saying: "These men, being Jews, disturb our city."

Then the people rose against them, their garments were torn off, and the magistrates commanded them to be beaten with rods, and then to be thrown into prison. At midnight, Paul and Silas were praying and praising God, and suddenly there was a great earthquake, so that the walls of the prison were shaken to their foundations. Immediately the doors flew open, and the bonds of the prisoners were released.

The keeper of the prison awaking in terror from his sleep, and seeing the doors open, drew his sword to kill himself, because he thought that the prisoners had fled. But Paul cried out to him: "Do thyself no harm, for we are all here!" Then the jailer, calling for a light, went in trembling, and fell down at the feet of Paul and Silas.

Then he brought them out, and said to them: "Masters, what must I do that I be saved?" They answered: "Believe in the Lord Jesus, and thou shalt be saved." That same hour he took them and washed their wounds; and he and all his household were baptized. Next morning the magistrates sent orders to the jailer to release Paul and Silas, but when they learned that the two apostles were Roman citizens, they came themselves to ask pardon for having ill-treated them.

Bible Studies

After this, Paul and his companion visited many cities of Macedonia. From there Paul went to Athens, the most celebrated city of Greece. Seeing that city wholly given up to idolatry, his heart was stirred within him; he disputed publicly in the synagogues with the Jews, and in the market-place everyday with all who were present.

Then came to Paul certain philosophers, who conducted him to Areopagus, saying: "May we know what this new doctrine is, which thou speakest of?" And Paul, standing in the midst of the Areopagus, said: "Ye men of Athens, passing, and seeing your idols, I found an altar on which was written: 'To the unknown God.' "What, therefore, you worship without knowing it, this I preach to you." He then preached to them the doctrine of Jesus Christ, but only a few of them believed. Among these few was Dionysius the Areopagite, one of the most learned men of his time. After Paul had preached the gospel at Athens, he went to Corinth.

There he preached first to the Jews, but they would not hear him, but rather blasphemed and contradicted all that he said. Then Paul, filled with a holy indignation, spoke to them: "Your blood be upon your own heads; I am clean. From henceforth I will go to the Gentiles." He then preached to the pagans of Corinth, many of whom were converted. Having remained in Corinth a year and six months, teaching and preaching, he returned to Antioch.

Question 7   ❖   How did Saint Paul escape jail?
Question 8   ❖   Did many of the Greeks from Athens convert?
Question 9   ❖   What was decided at the Council of Jerusalem?

Level 5 - Lesson 12

Saints

Saint Alphonsus Liguori

Alphonsus was the eldest son of a naval officer, and was born at his father's country house near Naples in 1696. He was never sent to school, but was educated by tutors at home, so that his father could be sure that he worked properly at his lessons. As well as his lessons, he practiced the harpsichord, the piano of those days, for three hours a day, and by the time he was thirteen could play like a master. All his life he had a great love for music, and later on he wrote and composed many hymns.

His father had determined that he should become a lawyer, and, as Alphonsus had a keen brain and was a good speaker, he enjoyed working hard for that too. He worked so hard, in fact, that he became a Doctor of Laws when he was only sixteen, though, as a rule, no one was allowed to do this before they were twenty. He was at the time so small that he could hardly be seen in his doctor's robes, and all the people laughed at him. But they did not laugh long. By the time he was just over twenty he was one of the leading lawyers in Naples.

In the year 1723 there was a great lawsuit between the Grand Duke of Tuscany and a nobleman of Naples about some property worth a hundred thousand pounds. Alphonsus, who, they said, had never lost a case, was the leading lawyer on one side, and after he had made a brilliant opening speech he sat down, quite sure he had won again, and waiting for the witnesses to be called. But his opponent did not call any witnesses. He just said, "Your arguments are a waste of breath. You have overlooked a document which destroys your whole case."

"What document is that?" said Alphonsus. "Let me see it."

His opponent handed him the paper, and when Alphonsus read it he turned pale. It was nothing new. It was something he had read over and over again, but he saw now that he had thought it meant exactly the opposite of what it did mean.

"You are right," he said. "I made a mistake. This document gives you the case."

He left the law court almost in tears. He thought his career would be ruined. People would imagine not that he, the most brilliant of the lawyers of Naples, had made a careless mistake, but that he had really been deceitful and bribed by the other side. He swore that he would never appear as a lawyer again, and for three days he would neither eat anything nor see anyone.

Then he realized that perhaps this humiliation had been sent by God to break his pride, and that God wanted him to serve Him in some special way. He prayed a great deal that he might know God's will, and one day when he was visiting the sick in the Hospital for Incurables, which he did every week and he was given the answer. He found himself surrounded by a mysterious light; the house seemed to shake, and he heard a voice in his heart saying, "Leave the world, and give yourself to Me." This happened twice, and when he had finished his visit he went straight to a church, laid his sword before a statue of Our Lady, and promised to become a priest.

Saints

He was only twenty-six at the time. He was ordained priest at the age of thirty, and he lived until he was ninety-one the kind of life he promised to lead, one in which he would never waste a single minute.

His first work was to teach the peasants in the country districts, and this led to the founding of a new Order in the Church – the Congregation of the Most Holy Redeemer, who are generally known as the Redemptorists.

Then, when he was fifty-six, the Pope insisted on making him Bishop of a diocese lying just off the road between Naples and Capua, known as Saint Agatha of the Goths, which, in spite of illness which in the end left him paralyzed, he ruled till he was nearly eighty. And, in spite of all the work he had to do among people who did not really know about the Faith or want to lead good lives, he managed to write book after book, and use all the learning he had and his sharp, trained lawyer's mind and his love of music for the glory of God.

Saint Alphonsus Liguori's Feast Day is August 2nd.

Question 10 ◈ What sign did Saint Alphonsus receive which made him become a priest?
Question 11 ◈ What religious Order did Saint Alphonsus found?
Question 12 ◈ What was the name of the Religious Order of nuns started by Saint Vincent de Paul?

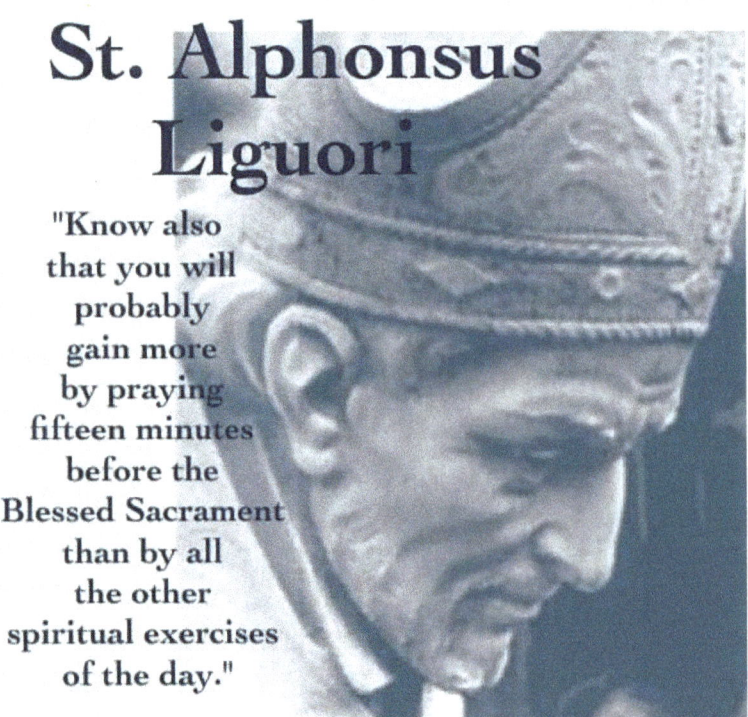

Confirmation

Christian Perfection

Should we be satisfied merely to keep the commandments of God?

We should not be satisfied merely to keep the commandments of God, but should always be ready to do good deeds, even when they are not commanded.

1) If we only give God what He commands us to give, we would be doing only what is absolutely necessary. In such a case we would go to church only once a week, plus five holy days of obligation a year; we would go to Confession only once a year, and receive Holy Communion only during the Easter Time. By doing these things and avoiding all serious violation of the Commandments, we would still be obeying God and keeping ourselves from mortal sin and saving our souls.

What would you think if a child who gives to his parents only what is demanded of him? What would you think of him if he never showed them any affection, never did anything extra for them to show his love and gratitude? We would say he is an abnormal son, an unnatural child.

2) We say that we love God, our Creator, Father, and Friend, our Saviour, the Source of all our benefits and graces. Love is proved by deeds, by the amount of sacrifice we would be willing to make for the beloved person. This is why we know Christ the God-Man loved us so much: He sacrificed everything, life itself, for us. Can we ever return such love? Can we ever serve God sufficiently, to show our affection?

He does not command us to go out of our way to help the poor; but can we consider anyone a good Christian who does not do so? A Christian should not only obey the commands of Christ, but should follow His counsels.

We go to church on weekdays, because we love Him, and wish to visit Him in the Most Blessed Sacrament of the altar, to receive Him into our very hearts. We should think up extra things to do for God, as we think up extra things to do for the person we love most. Our parents do not command us to buy gifts for them on their birthdays; but if we do so, are they not delighted at our show of affection?

Level 5 - Lesson 12

Confirmation

What does Christian perfection consist of?

Christian perfection consists in union with God by the practice of virtue; it requires love of God and our neighbor, and detachment of the heart from the things of this world.

1) Christian perfection is nothing else but sanctity, holiness, the love of the saints for God. Lest those who call themselves 'ordinary mortals' be afraid to aspire to this sanctity, we must make it clear that it does not require deep, abiding love, for "Love is the fulfilling of the law," the fulfillment of it to its very foundation and depths, not merely on the surface.

2) God requires all to aspire to Christian perfection. He says: "You therefore are to be perfect, even as your heavenly Father is perfect".

3) All states of life can be sanctified by those who wish only to live for God. Saints are found in every class. Love of God is in everybody's power.

4) The model of Christian perfection is Our Lord. The saints, who imitated Him steadfastly, are also patterns of perfection.

    (a) We should begin from youth to strive after perfection
    (b) Everyone should choose for his model a saint whose position and calling are similar to his own.

5) In order to be in the state of Christian perfection, we must have a spirit of detachment towards the things of this world.

Let us remember that the eternal is what counts; the temporal is given us by God only to help us fulfill our end of praising, of serving Him, and thus saving our soul.

Question 13   What is meant by striving for Christian perfection?
Question 14   What do we need to be in the state of perfection?
Question 15   How do we acquire the fruits of the Holy Ghost?

Church History

The Crusades

In the early centuries, many Christians liked to make pilgrimages to the Church which housed the true Cross and other places in the Holy Land connected with the life and death of Christ.
In 637 the Arabs, now Moslems, captured Jerusalem. They allowed Christian pilgrims to visit the Holy places, but forced them to pay heavy taxes, and treated them very badly.
In 1073, the Turks, then also Moslems, over-ran the whole of Palestine and conditions became much worse for pilgrims. This, for Christians, was a very sad state of affairs to see the desecration of the Holy places, and to hear of the suffering of the Christian pilgrim.

Peter the Hermit, a monk from France, persuaded Pope Urban II to rally the Christian Princes of Europe to send armies to rescue these Holy places from the hands of the Moslem's.
From 1093 to 1274, there were five major Crusades, as they were called, led by Christian kings and princes of Europe, and one by Saint Bernard. These Crusaders for Christ wore a Cross on their cloaks. The Crusades failed on the whole, but they succeeded in holding back the Moslems armies, preventing them from overrunning Europe for two centuries.

Jerusalem remained in the hands of the Turks until the Great War of 1914 – 1918.

Question 16   Why were the Crusades thought to be necessary?
Question 17   How many major Crusades were there?
Question 18   In what year did the East go into open schism with Rome?

St. Francis of Assisi in the Dream of Pope Innocent III – Giotto

Lesson 13

Level 5

Confirmation

Catechism

The Holy Eucharist

157. Did anything of the bread and wine remain after they had been changed into Our Lord's body and blood?

After the bread and wine had been changed into Our Lord's body and blood, there remained only the appearances of bread and wine.

158. What do we mean by the appearances of bread and wine?

By the appearances of bread and wine we mean the color, taste, weight, and shape.

159. When did Christ give His priests the power to change bread and wine into His body and blood?

Christ gave His priests the power to change bread and wine into His body and blood when He said to the apostles at the Last Supper: "Do this in remembrance of Me."

The Blessed Sacrament is such a wonderful thing! To think that Our Lord came down from heaven, offered His life for us, and if that wasn't enough, He comes to our altars every time the priest utters the sacred words of Consecration. He rests in our tabernacles waiting for us to visit Him and He gives Himself to us in Holy Communion.

It is easy to see how much God loves us, but it is more difficult to understand how Jesus is present in the Holy Eucharist. The three catechism questions of this lesson are extremely important. Learn them well. They do not fully explain the miracle (for how can we fully explain a miracle?), but they teach us what happens to the bread and wine at the Consecration. The actual bread (substance) changes into the Body, Blood, Soul and Divinity of Jesus, while the appearance (accidents) remain the same. We will spend our whole lives contemplating this mystery as did the saints, but the most important thing is that we believe it and come to love our dear Saviour more and more.

Question 1 ❖ Did anything of the bread and wine remain after they had been changed into Our Lord's body and blood?

Question 2 ❖ When did Christ give His priests the power to change bread and wine into His body and blood?

Question 3 ❖ What is the Holy Eucharist?

Level 5 - Lesson 13

Prayer

Prayer to the Holy Ghost

The Prayer to the Holy Ghost is usually said before lessons or meetings. He is invoked also before great decisions are made. We sometimes forget to pray to the Holy Ghost, but He is ever with us, inspiring us and flooding our souls with graces when we need them.

Come O Holy Ghost, fill the hearts of Thy faithful

In this prayer, we are invoking the third Person of the Blessed Trinity. We are asking Him to fill our souls with His grace and His gifts, and the souls of our neighbors.

And enkindle in them the fire of Thy love

We also ask for the grace of our loving God with the intensity that God loves us. We ask that this fire be lit within us that we might produce the fruits of the Holy Ghost.

Question 4 ❖ What are we asking of the Holy Ghost in this prayer?
Question 5 ❖ When is the Prayer to the Holy Ghost usually said?
Question 6 ❖ What is the difference between the first and second time we pray to the heavenly court?

Bible Studies

Saint Paul's Third Mission (AD 55 to 58)

After Paul had remained some time at Antioch, he passed a second time through the greater part of Asia Minor, and came to Ephesus, the capital of the Roman province of Asia. Here he met some twelve disciples, and said to them: "Have you received the Holy Ghost?" They answered him: "We have not so much as heard whether there be a Holy Ghost."

Paul asked them again: "In what then were you baptized?" They replied: "In John's baptism." Then Paul said: "John baptized the people with the baptism of penance, saying that they should believe in Him who was to come after him, that is to say: Jesus." Hearing this, they were baptized in the name of the Lord Jesus. Then Paul laid his hands upon them, and they received the Holy Ghost.

Paul remained two years at Ephesus, so that all those who dwelt in the Roman province of Asia heard the word of the Lord. Moreover, God was pleased to work many wonderful miracles by the hand of the holy apostle, and no sooner were handkerchiefs or aprons that had touched his body, applied to the sick than they were instantly cured. Seeing these things, a great fear came upon all the people, and they magnified the name of Jesus.

Many of those who had dealt in the magic art brought their books, which were of great value, and burned them before the apostle and the whole people. But a certain man named Demetrius, a silversmith, who made little idols and miniature models in silver of the famous temple of Diana called together his fellow craftsmen and told them that Paul by his preaching, was destroying their trade, turning the people away from the worship of Diana, on which their living depended.

When the silversmiths heard this, they cried out: "Great is Diana of the Ephesians!" And a tumult was raised throughout the whole city. The people were about to lay hold on Paul and his disciples, with intent to kill them; but, happily, the town clerk, by wise persuasions, succeeded in appeasing their wrath, so that peace was speedily restored.

The tumult being quelled, Paul assembled the Christians of Ephesus, and having exhorted them to persevere, sailed for Macedonia. Then he went to Troas, where he remained for seven days. On Sunday, he assembled all the faithful in an upper chamber, where he offered up the Holy Sacrifice and preached to the people till midnight.

The sermon being so long, a young man named Eutychus, who sat in the window, having fallen asleep, fell from the third story to the ground, and was taken up as dead. Paul hearing of the accident, immediately went down and restored the young man to life. From Troas, Paul repaired to Lesbos, Chios, Samos, and Miletus. From the latter place he sent for the clergy of Ephesus, and bade them a last tender farewell, saying: "Now, behold, bound in the spirit, I go to Jerusalem, not knowing the things that shall befall me there." He then told them that he feared nothing, but was willing to lay down his life for his divine Master.

Level 5 - Lesson 13

Bible Studies

To the bishops he said: "Take heed to yourselves, and to all the flock over which the Holy Ghost has placed you bishops to rule the Church of God, which He hath purchased with His own blood. I know that after my departure, ravenous wolves will enter among you, not sparing the flock." Then, kneeling down, he prayed with them all. And there was much weeping among them; and, falling on Paul's neck, they embraced him, and accompanied him to the ship, sorrowing that they should see his face no more.

Question 7 ❖ How long did Saint Paul remain at Ephesus?
Question 8 ❖ Explain why the people were about to lay hold of St Paul in Ephesus?
Question 9 ❖ How did Saint Paul escape jail?

Saints

Saint Therese of Lisieux

Nothing could have been more different from the poor home of Saint Bernadette Soubirous than that large, comfortable house of Therese Martin. Mr. Martin was a wealthy watchmaker, who, when his wife died, leaving him with five girls (of whom Therese was the youngest), retired to the town of Lisieux; and there in a big house standing in a great garden with lawns and flowers and trees he settled down to bring up his children.

Therese and her sisters, Marie, Pauline, Leonie, and Celine, were able to have most of the things they wanted; but their father brought them up to understand that what they should want most of all was to please God; and when Pauline was twenty-one she decided to become a nun in the Carmelite convent at Lisieux. When ten year-old Therese heard this she started to cry very bitterly. Pauline was her "little mother," who had brought her up after their mother died; Pauline was her favorite sister; but above all, ever since she could remember she and Pauline had played at being hermits and had always said they would go away together and now Pauline was going alone and leaving her.

But she had to wait only five years before she joined Pauline again, and herself became a nun in the Carmelite convent of the town. That was a very early age for anyone to enter; but her father was willing that she should go, and when she and her father and her sister Celine were on a visit to Rome she actually asked the Pope, "Holy Father," she asked, as she knelt before him in audience, "I have a great favor to ask. In honor of your Jubilee, allow me to become a Carmelite when I am fifteen." "My child," said the Pope, "you must do as the Superiors decide."

"Holy Father," persisted Therese, "if only you will say yes everyone else will agree". "If it be God's will," said the Pope, "you shall enter", and three months after her fifteenth birthday she entered.

Ten years later she died, and if it had not been that her sister Pauline, who was prioress for some of the time, had ordered her to write her autobiography we would know nothing about her life. This book shows how she tried to live and all about her "Little Way," as it is called. This meant that she tried to please God in the very smallest things of her life, but she understood that everything that happened to her was His will and His gift. If she were scolded she would not answer back. If she had any sorrow or disappointment she would not show it. She changed a pretty jug in her cell for an ugly, cracked one, because another Sister liked hers. However ill or tired she felt, she would never complain. When she was dying she said: "I feel that my mission is soon to begin, to teach my Little Way to souls. I want to spend my heaven in doing good on earth. There can be no rest for me till the end of the world."

Almost as soon as she was dead many miracles happened, and the world knew that the girl who had always tried "never to refuse God anything" was a saint.

Saint Therese's Feast Day is October 3rd.

Question 10 ❖ What convent did Saint Therese enter and in what town?
Question 11 ❖ What do we mean by the 'Little Way' of Saint Therese?
Question 12 ❖ What sign did Saint Alphonsus receive which made him become a priest?

Confirmation

General Means of Perfection

What are the general means of perfection? After the observance of the Commandments of God and of the Church, the general means of perfection are:

1) **Faithfullness :** By faithfulness in small things, we obtain greater graces and avoid grave sins more easily. As in the natural order, so in the spiritual, great things come from apparently insignificant things. We should be careful to avoid venial sins in order to be saved from mortal sins.

2) **Self-control and self-denial :** Self-control and self-denial are acts of mortification: keeping down anger, and abstaining even from things which are permitted, but above all avoiding even the least yielding to what is forbidden. Self-control is the mark of the true Christian. If we deny ourselves some things which are permitted, we shall find it easier to avoid what is forbidden. Self-control gives us a strong will. Self-denial is the mark of the human being made to the likeness of God; a beast does not say "No" to himself.

3) **Order and Regularity:** We observe order and regularity by having a fixed time for everything; for rising, retiring, eating, work, recreation, etc.

4) **A habit of Prayer :** By prayer we shall avoid temptations and obtain blessings. We should especially make a habit of aspiration prayers.

5) **A frequent recourse to solitude :** Solitude helps us grow in virtue. The noise and bustle of the world are distractions. We should once in a while imitate Our Lord and withdraw into solitude, to see our faults better, and get closer to God.

6) **Reading spiritual books and mediation :** We should have some regular spiritual reading and meditation, even if for only ten minutes every day, as food for our souls.

7) **Frequentation of the sacraments :** God instituted the sacraments as effective means of grace. We should have recourse to the sacraments of Penance and Holy Eucharist as often as we reasonably can. Can we get more grace than from God Himself, coming in Holy Communion?

Question 13 ◆ Why does solitude help us grow in virtue?
Question 14 ◆ What is the first general means of perfection?
Question 15 ◆ What is meant by striving for Christian perfection?

Level 5 - Lesson 13

Church History

Popes of the Ninth Century to the Thirteenth

This period of time was known as the Middle Ages or Medieval Times. Throughout Europe, there were princes and lords who owned large tracts of land, which were divided up among tenants who worked the lands and lived off them, and gave various services to the community, and paid the owners usually in produce or service. They in turn were responsible for the safety and general welfare of all. Safety was a very big factor. This system was known as the Feudal System.

As a result of this system, Bishops and Monasteries turned for protection, to the secular power of the Kings and Princes. Over the years the Church acquired much property and had therefore secular responsibilities as well as spiritual.

Eventually, Kings and Princes, Lords and Barons, appointed Abbots and Bishops of their own choice, not necessarily good and holy men. This was called 'Lay Investiture'. Even Popes were nominated and elected to suit the wishes of secular powers, and were insulted, imprisoned, even assassinated by their masters. It led also to Simony (the selling of Church Offices) as well as to neglect of spiritual values among Churchmen.

In the 9th and 10th centuries the Popes came under the power of Roman factions, headed by the Feudal princes of Italy. Eight Popes reigned for a year or less. Sometimes there were even two or more men claiming to be Pope at the same time. Pope Nicholas II called together the Lateran Council 1059, which decreed that Popes must be elected by Cardinal Bishops, in completely free elections.

Alexander II followed Nicholas II. He fought the great evils of the times, lay investiture, simony, and corruption of the clergy. He supported William the Conqueror in England, where there were good Churchmen like Anslem, Lanfranc and Thomas A'Beckett.

Pope Gregory VII became Pope in 1073. He continued the fight against Lay Investiture and State domination over the Church as well as attacking all other abuses.

The thirteenth century (1200-1300) opened with Innocent III as Pope. He, like Gregory VII, was one of the greatest Popes. He strongly defended truth and morality in every country. He regained for the Papacy an influence and a prestige greater than ever.

Church History

Innocent III appointed Stephen Langton, Archbishop of Canterbury, against the wishes of King John of England. This Archbishop and the Barons of England later forced King John to sign the 'Magna Carter'.

Innocent III called together the 4th Lateran Council in 1215. This Council defined the Doctrine of Transubstantiation (that the bread and wine at the Consecration of the Mass become really and truly the Body and Blood of Our Divine Lord). It also approved the Franciscan and Dominican Orders.

Innocent III became Pope at the age of 37. He died aged 55.

A most remarkable fact is that during all those sad times of the 9th and 10th centuries, the work of the Church continued on with success, and neither doctrine nor discipline suffered any great breakdown.

More about the Magna Carta

- It promised that laws would be good and fair
- Everyone shall have access to courts, that cost and money should not be a problem if any person wants to take their problem to the courts
- States that no freeman will be imprisoned or punished without going through the proper legal system

Question 16	❖	What do we mean by 'Lay Investiture'?
Question 17	❖	Who were two of the greatest Popes of the Middle Ages, in the Church?
Question 18	❖	What did the Lateran Council of 1059 decide?
Question 19	❖	How many major Crusades were there?

Lesson 14

Level 5

Confirmation

Catechism

The Holy Sacrifice of the Mass

160. What is the Mass?

The Mass is the sacrifice of the New Law in which Christ, through the priest, offers Himself to God in an unbloody manner under the appearance of bread and wine.

161. Is the Mass the same sacrifice as the sacrifice of the cross?

The Mass is the same sacrifice as the sacrifice of the cross.

162. Is there any difference between the sacrifice of the cross and the Sacrifice of the Mass?

The manner in which the sacrifice is offered is different. On the cross Christ physically shed His blood and was physically slain, while in the Mass there is no physical shedding of blood nor physical death.

When we go to Mass, we are actually at the foot of the Cross. Yes, the Mass is the same sacrifice of Jesus as it was on the Cross 2000 years ago. The only difference is that Jesus does not physically shed His Blood. But the sacrifice is the same. Our Lord Jesus Christ is still the victim.

There is nothing more sacred upon this earth than the Mass, especially the moment of the Consecration. In fact, every time we go to Mass, we witness a miracle; the changing of bread and wine into the Body, Blood, Soul and Divinity of Jesus Christ.
Oh how we should prepare for the Mass and with what reverence we should attend Mass!

Question 1 ❖ What is the Mass?
Question 2 ❖ Is the Mass the same sacrifice as the sacrifice of the cross?
Question 3 ❖ Did anything of the bread and wine remain after they had been changed into Our Lord's body and blood?

Level 5 - Lesson 14

Prayer

Prayer to the Holy Ghost

Send Forth Thy Spirit and thou shall be created

When we pray these words we are asking the Holy Ghost to give to us His gifts, His graces, that we may use them as He desires. The Holy Ghost is the love of God, and His grace is what animates our every good action. The Holy Ghost continually creates in us new and better Catholics. We need but ask the Holy Ghost for His graces and He will generously pour them upon us.

And Thou shall renew the face of the Earth

Our Lord once told His disciples that faith, the size of a mustard seed could move mountains. Saint Gregory the Wonder worker took Our Lord at His word and literally moved a mountain. When the Holy Ghost pours His graces upon us, we can change the world, we can indeed "renew the face of the earth".

Question 4 ❖ What is possible if we have a true faith?
Question 5 ❖ What are we asking of the Holy Ghost in this prayer?

Bible Studies

Last Years of the Life of the Apostles

When Paul had returned to Jerusalem, he was seized by the Jews and cast into prison. After two years' imprisonment he was sent, at his own request, to Rome, to be judged by the emperor. On his way to the great city he was shipwrecked at Malta, but was saved in a miraculous manner.

Arrived in Rome, He was kept two years more in prison, but having then obtained his freedom, he began to preach the gospel. At the same time the other apostles were journeying in various countries, preaching as they went, and working all manner of signs and prodigies. Peter, in his capacity of head of the Church, visited the different churches, confirming them in the faith.

It was with that intention that he had gone before Paul to the capital of the ancient world, and had there established his Episcopal See; he returned after each of his apostolic journeys, or visitations, and in his last years he remained there permanently.

Peter and the other apostles everywhere established bishops as their successors. These bishops were to govern the faithful, and to teach them the same doctrine that they had learned from the apostles. As to the scriptures of the New Testament, we must bear in mind that they were written later. Hence the apostles and the first followers of the apostles had no written books to convert the world. It was all done by preaching. The apostles preached what they had seen with their own eyes, and their successors preached what they had learned from the apostles. Much of what the apostles preached was written down in the books of the New Testament, but not all. Yet even the unwritten teaching has come down to us, and it is called tradition.

All the apostles, with one exception, sealed with their blood the gospel which they announced to the world. In the year of our Lord 67, Paul returned to Rome, were he and Peter gloriously suffered martyrdom under NerO. Paul, being a Roman citizen, was beheaded; Peter died on a cross, with his head downwards. James the Greater suffered under Herod, about the year 42 of the Christian era.

John, the beloved disciple, who had been thrown into a cauldron of boiling oil, and was miraculously preserved, was the only one who died a natural death, about the year 100. The successors of the apostles were no less zealous for the truth than their masters had been; most of them sealed their faith with their blood. Yet the Church was not abandoned.

The bishops continued with unwearying zeal the work which the holy apostles had commenced. As the faithful were obedient to their bishops, so the bishops were obedient to the successor of Saint Peter, that is, the Pope of Rome, who is the chief pastor of the Church. In this manner there was a bond of union and unity between the faithful and their priests, between the priests and their bishops, and between all the bishops and the Pope. Thus was established the One, Holy, Catholic, and Apostolic Church, which, built by Christ upon the rock of Peter, and guided by the Holy Ghost, has now existed for twenty centuries, and shall exist till the end of time, in spite of all that the infernal powers can do against it. Happy are they that belong to that Church, who believe as she believes, and who do the works which she prescribes.

Level 5 - Lesson 14

Bible Studies

Question 6 ❖ What did Saint Peter and the other Apostles establish everywhere and why?
Question 7 ❖ How, where and when did Saints Peter and Paul die?
Question 8 ❖ Who was the only apostle not to suffer martyrdom?
Question 9 ❖ How long did Saint Paul remain at Ephesus?

Matthew was the former tax-collector turned evangelist. He suffered martyrdom in Ethiopia and was killed by a halberd (combined spear and battleaxe).

Simon the Zealot's death is shrouded in uncertainty, yet early accounts record that he was either crucified in the Kingdom of Iberia, Samaria, or Persia.

Peter was crucified upside down. Apparently, it was because he told his tormentors that he felt unworthy to die in the same way that Jesus Christ had died.

Philip was believed to be martyred in the ancient Greek city of Hierapolis, where he was impaled by iron hooks and hanged upside down to die. In 2011 his tomb was officially found.

John was boiled in oil, but miraculously delivered from death. He died peacefully while living in exile in Patmos (where he wrote the Book of Revelation).

James the Just, the leader of the church in Jerusalem, was thrown off the Temple wall when he refused to deny his faith. Having survived, his enemies killed him with a club.

Judas (Thaddeus) was martyred in Persia on his missionary journey where he was hewed with an axe by religious leaders (Magi).

Andrew was crucified in Greece. After being whipped severely, they tied his body to a cross. He continued to preach to his tormentors for two days until he expired.

James the Great was otherwise known as one of the Son's of Thunder. He evangelised Spain and is the Patron Saint of that nation. He was beheaded by Herod.

Bartholomew, also known as Nathaniel, was a missionary to Asia and present day Turkey. He was martyred in Armenia where he was flayed to death by a whip.

Thomas, of the doubting Thomas fame, was stabbed with spears in India during one of his missionary trips where he established the church in the sub-continent.

Matthias was chosen to replace Judas Iscariot. Matthias worked amongst cannibals. Records of his death vary, some record stoning/beheading/crucifixion.

Saints

Saint Elizabeth of Hungary

Saint Elizabeth of Hungary, or, as she is sometimes called, Saint Elizabeth of Thuringia, is still known to the Germans as their 'dear Saint Elizabeth,' and is one of the best loved of all their saints. She was the daughter of one of the kings of Hungary, but when she was only four the powerful ruler of Thuringia asked her father if she might be brought up at his court, which at that time was one of the most brilliant in Europe, and, when she grew up, marry his son. So, when she was just a child, Elizabeth went to live in splendor in the great castle of the Wartburg among the poets and the 'Minnesingers' whom the King liked to have around him. The Prince whom one day she was to marry, whose name was Ludwig, was a boy of nine, and from that very first moment they met the children became the dearest of friends. They were married when Elizabeth was fifteen and Ludwig twenty, in the year that the old ruler died and Ludwig became King in his place.

During her girlhood, Elizabeth was so devoted to religion that she was sometimes laughed at by the more worldly people at court. One day there was a great service in the Church of Saint Catherine at Eisenach which was always attended by the royal family in much pomp. During this, Princess Elizabeth suddenly left her place and put the crown she was wearing at the foot of the great crucifix. Her mother-in-law, who was shocked by this breach of etiquette, whispered to her that this was not the time or the place to do such a thing, and ordered her to put the crown on again. But Elizabeth, in tears, answered: "Dear lady mother, please do not scold me. Here I see Jesus, Who died for me, wearing His crown of thorns. How can I wear in His presence this crown of gold and gems? My crown seems a mockery of His!"

When Elizabeth herself became Queen, her husband was called away to attend the Emperor on a journey to Italy, and that year terrible storms and floods, causing famine and plague, burst on Thuringia. Though she was only nineteen, Elizabeth insisted on taking charge of everything personally. Each day a certain quantity of bread was baked in the palace, and she herself served it out to the poor who came to the gates of the Wartburg, giving them all a just share. In this way, by what today we call 'rationing,' she managed to see that no one actually starved, and when the autumn came she sent the people into the harvest fields with scythes and sickles, and to every man she gave a shirt and a pair of new shoes.

To deal with those who were sick she had a special hospital built below the Wartburg, in which there were twenty-eight beds. She herself visited it daily to attend to the needs of the patients. In order to have money for them, and for alms she distributed throughout the whole of Ludwig's territory, she sold her jewels and her beautiful clothes, and even some of the State robes. This made some of the selfish courtiers very angry, but when Ludwig came home again he said she had been quite right, and he confirmed everything she had done in his absence.

Ludwig soon had to leave her again, this time to go on a Crusade. But before he got as far as the Holy Land he caught a fever and died. As he was dying he commanded his knights and counts who stood around his bed that they should carry his body to his native land and defend his Elizabeth and their children, with their life blood, if necessary from all wrong and oppression. When the news arrived at the Wartburg Elizabeth cried: "Now all the world and its joys are dead to me!" and fainted from grief.

Ludwig's brother, Henry, decided that he would now become ruler of Thuringia instead of Herman, the little son of Ludwig and Elizabeth; and in the depth of winter she and her children were forced to leave the Wartburg.

Level 5 - Lesson 14

Saints

Henry forbade anyone in the neighborhood to take her in, because he was afraid it might lead to a revolt against him; but at last she found some kind people in an inn who allowed her to stay there, and for some weeks she supported herself and her children by spinning wool.

But before long the knights and counts got back to Thuringia with Ludwig's body, and they remembered their vow to their dead king. They forced Henry to be content with the title of Regent: they put young Herman on the throne as King; and they saw to it that Elizabeth was given the city of Marburg as her own property. Elizabeth's own relatives suggested that, as she was still only twenty, she should marry again. But this she refused absolutely. She had loved only Ludwig as long as she could remember anything, and no one, she swore, should be allowed to take his place.

At that time Saint Francis of Assisi had just founded his new Order of poor preachers, living a life of charity and poverty; and it was to them that Elizabeth turned. She wished to join them and herself become a beggar; but her confessor forbade her to, although he said she might become a member of the Third Order of Saint Francis, which was meant for those who still lived ordinary lives in the world.

So she built a great Franciscan hospital at Marburg, and devoted herself entirely to the care of the sick for the few years of life that were left her. She died when she was only twenty-four.

They buried her in the church attached to her hospital, and after her death so many miracles were worked there that it became a place of pilgrimage in Europe, almost as famous as the shrine of Saint James at Compostela in Spain. And within four years of the death of 'the greatest woman of the Middle Ages,' as she has been called, a great church at Marburg was built and dedicated to Saint Elizabeth.

Saint Elizabeth's Feast Day is November 19th.

Question 10 ❖ What is Saint Elizabeth most remembered for?
Question 11 ❖ What did Saint Elizabeth do in the last few years of her life?
Question 12 ❖ What do we mean by the 'Little Way' of Saint Therese?

Confirmation

General Means of Perfection – Self Denial

What are the three principal degrees in self-denial?

1) An habitual disposition to lose all things, even life itself, and suffer all things rather than commit a mortal sin.
This first degree of self-denial is necessary for all in order to be saved. Our Lord said, "Whosoever doth not carry his cross, and come after me, cannot be my disciple." Our ordinary cross, the cross of all men, is our human tendency to weakness, to fall into sin; against this tendency we must all battle to acquire the first degree of perfection, of self-denial.

2) An habitual disposition to lose and suffer all, rather than commit a deliberate venial sin.
This second degree is a mark of affection towards God: we avoid even small faults because they displease Him. It is those in this second disposition that are very active in good works, trying to do all they can for the glory of God, out of love for God, and for their fellow men for God's sake. They set a good example to others by their good works, according to the words of Scripture: "A city set on a mountain cannot be hidden. So let your light shine before men in order that they may see your good works, and give glory to your Father in heaven" (Matt. 5:14, 16).

3) An habitual disposition to prefer being poor, forgotten, despised, and suffering, - with Jesus on the Cross, in order to resemble Him more, as a proof of love, - rather than rich, honored and praised, full of delights and consolations.
This third degree is the acme of perfection; it is sanctity. By this disposition, one becomes a fool for Christ's sake. Suppose that God has given you wealth, honors, talents, and all other worldly blessings, and assures you that with them all, enjoying them all, you can still reach the same place in heaven that you can without them. And yet, just to resemble Jesus, who was poor and despised and tortured, you joyfully choose to give up all your worldly blessings.

Question 13	❖	List the three degrees in self-denial.
Question 14	❖	What is meant by self-denial?
Question 15	❖	What is the first general means of perfection?

Level 5 - Lesson 14

Church History

The Avignon Popes - The Western Schism

The Holy Catholic Church is the longest surviving institution since the Birth of Christ, and on God's Word will last until the end of the world. It has been beset with numberless difficulties in various ages, as is happening today, but always she survives the human element that would destroy her in purely human institutions. In our Church History lessons so far, we have seen the dreadful persecutions in the Roman times and the threat of Islamic domination. From within the Church itself, there were various heresies, the worst perhaps being the Arian heresy that denied the Divinity of Christ.

After the Barbarian invasions of Europe, there were the difficulties of political and various national interests. Our last lesson took us through the difficulties that beset the Papacy through to the thirteenth century, during the Middle Ages. In this lesson we follow the further difficulties up to 1414.

At the end of the Thirteenth century, owing to the continual turmoil in Rome, the Popes were inclined to be absent from Rome, and to be in some of the neighboring cities.

In 1309 Pope Clement V (1305 – 1314) finally left Rome and went to live in Avignon in France. Succeeding Popes lived there until 1377. This period of just 70 years brought many troubles to the Church.

The transfer of Church Administration from Rome had serious results. In Rome, the Pope was a sovereign independent ruler. At Avignon, though independent, the Pope came too much under the influence of France. The move from his own See of Rome weakened the international character of the Papacy, which had made it such a powerful influence for order and peace in the reign of Innocent III. The Avignon Popes, by choosing French officials for the Church, also provoked the hostility and suspicion of other countries.

Deprived of their Italian revenues in Avignon, the popes had to raise taxes on Church property throughout Europe. This brought them into conflict with the bishops and rulers of other countries. The 100 years war between England and France (1338 – 1438) and the Black Death plague of 1347, did not help the Avignon Popes, and caused death, devastation, and disorder throughout Europe.

In 1377 Gregory IX at last yielding to the entreaties of Saint Catherine of Siena. (1347 – 1380) returned to Rome. After the death of Pope Gregory IX, the people of Rome demanded an Italian Pope. The Cardinals elected Urban VI, an Italian. He offended the French so much they elected another Pope. He called himself Clement VII and lived at Avignon.

Church History

This threw the Church into confusion with one Pope in Rome, another in Avignon. This was the beginning of the Great Western Schism, which lasted from 1378 until 1414. During this time there were two Popes, each claiming to be the true Pope.

In 1414 the Council of Constance elected Pope Martin V. He was accepted by all the parties as the one, true Pope. The great Schism was ended, and the Church was once more united under the one head: Martin V.

Question 16 ❖ What decision about the Papacy was made at Lateran Council?
Question 17 ❖ What Council marked the end of 'The great Schism'?
Question 18 ❖ Which pope, at the entreaties of Saint Catherine returned to Rome?

Artist: St. Giovanni di Paolo. *Catherine before the Pope at Avignon.*
Catherine expressed profound devotion. Among other stories is that of the visit that she paid to Pope Gregory XI in Avignon, during which she persuaded the curia to move back to its traditional residence in Rome.

Lesson 15

Level 5

Confirmation

Catechism

This is the last lesson of the year and is different to all other lessons as there are no new questions, nor is there any new work to learn, nor is there a test to complete. It is a summary of all you have learned this year. It gives you the opportunity to review all the things you have already studied, so that you have a better knowledge of your work and you will therefore be more pleasing to God.

14. **Is there only one God?**

    Yes, there is only one God.

15. **How many Persons are there in God?**

    In God there are three Divine Persons – the Father, the Son, and the Holy Ghost.

16. **What do we mean by the Blessed Trinity?**

    By the Blessed Trinity we mean one and the same God in three Divine Persons.

16a **How are the three Divine Persons, though really distinct from one another, one and the same God?**

    The three Divine Persons, though really distinct from one another, are one and the same God, because all have one and the same Divine Nature.

16b **Can we fully understand how the three Divine Persons, though really distinct from one another, are one and the same God?**

    We cannot fully understand how the three Divine Persons, though really distinct from one another, are one and the same God, because this is a supernatural mystery.

40. **Did God abandon man after Adam fell into sin?**

    God did not abandon man after Adam fell into sin, but promised to send into the world a Saviour to free man from his sins and to reopen to him the gates of heaven.

41. **Who is the Saviour of all men?**

    The Saviour of all men is Jesus Christ.

42. **What is the chief teaching of the Catholic Church about Jesus Christ?**

    The chief teaching of the Catholic Church about Jesus Christ is that He is God made man.

Catechism

43. **Is Jesus Christ more than one Person?**

No, Jesus Christ is only one Person; and that Person is the second Person of the Blessed Trinity.

44. **How many natures has Jesus Christ?**

*Jesus Christ has two natures: the nature of God and the nature of man.
(A nature is what someone is, A person is who someone is).*

45. **When was Christ born?**

Christ was born of the Blessed Virgin Mary on Christmas Day, in Bethlehem, more than two thousand years ago.

45a **What is meant by the Incarnation?**

By the Incarnation is meant that the Son of God, retaining His Divine nature, took to Himself a human nature, that is, a body and soul like ours.

45b **How was the Son of God made man?**

The Son of God was conceived and made man by the power of the Holy Ghost in the womb of the Blessed Virgin Mary.

45c **On what day did the Son of God become man?**

The Son of God became man on the twenty-fifth of March, the day of the Annunciation.

45d **Is Saint Joseph the father of Jesus Christ?**

Jesus Christ has no human father, but Saint Joseph was the spouse of the Blessed Virgin Mary and the guardian, or foster father of Jesus Christ.

45e **What is a supernatural mystery?**

A supernatural mystery is a truth we cannot fully understand, but which we firmly believe because we have God's word for it.

46. **What is meant by the redemption?**

By the redemption is meant that Jesus Christ offered His sufferings and death to God in satisfaction for the sins of men.

Catechism

47. **What do we learn from the sufferings and death of Christ?**

    From the sufferings and death of Christ we learn God's love for man and the evil of sin.

48. **What do we mean when we say in the Apostles' Creed that Christ descended into hell?**

    When we say that Christ descended into hell we mean that, after He died, the soul of Christ descended into a place or state of rest, called limbo, where the souls of the just were waiting for Him.

49. **When did Christ rise from the dead?**

    Christ rose from the dead, glorious and immortal, on Easter Sunday, the third day after His death.

50. **When did Christ ascend into heaven?**

    Christ ascended, body and soul, into heaven on Ascension Day, forty days after His Resurrection.

51. **What do we mean when we say that Christ sits at the right hand of God, the Father Almighty?**

    When we say that Christ sits at the right hand of God, the Father Almighty, we mean that Our Lord as God is equal to the Father, and that as man He has the highest place in heaven, next to God.

52. **What do we mean when we say that Christ will come from thence to judge the living and the dead?**

    When we say that Christ will come from thence to judge the living and the dead, we mean that on the last day Our Lord will come to judge everyone who has ever lived in this world.

138. **What is a sacrament?**

    A sacrament is an outward sign instituted by Christ to give grace.

139. **How many sacraments are there?**

    There are seven sacraments: Baptism, Confirmation, Holy Eucharist, Penance, Extreme Unction, Holy Orders, and Matrimony.

Level 5 - Lesson 14

Catechism

140. Do the sacraments give sanctifying grace?

The sacraments do give sanctifying grace.

141. Does each of the sacraments also give a special grace?

Each of the sacraments also gives a special grace, called sacramental grace.

142. Do the sacraments always give grace?

The sacraments always give grace if we receive them properly.

143. Why are Baptism and Penance called sacraments of the dead?

Baptism and Penance are called sacraments of the dead because their chief purpose is to give the life of grace to souls dead through sin.

144. Why are Confirmation, Holy Eucharist, Extreme Unction, Holy Orders, and Matrimony called sacraments of the living?

Confirmation, Holy Eucharist, Extreme Unction, Holy Orders, and Matrimony are called sacraments of the living because their chief purpose is to give more grace to souls already alive through grace.

145. What sin does he commit who knowingly receives a sacrament of the living in mortal sin?

He who knowingly receives a sacrament of the living in mortal sin commits a mortal sin of sacrilege.

146. Why can Baptism, Confirmation, and Holy Orders be received only once?

Baptism, Confirmation, and Holy Orders can be received only once because they imprint on the soul a spiritual mark which lasts forever.

147. What is Baptism?

Baptism is the sacrament that gives our souls the new life of grace by which we become children of God.

Catechism

148. What sin does Baptism take away?

Baptism takes away original sin; and also actual sins, if there be any, and all the punishment due to them.

149. Who can administer Baptism?

The priest is the usual minister of Baptism, but if there is danger that someone will die without Baptism, anyone else may and should baptize.

150. How would you give Baptism?

I would give Baptism by pouring ordinary water on the forehead of the person to be baptized, saying while pouring it: "I baptize thee in the name of the Father, and of the Son, and of the Holy Ghost."

151. What is Confirmation?

Confirmation is the sacrament through which the Holy Ghost comes to us in a special way and enables us to profess our faith as strong and perfect Christians and soldiers of Jesus Christ.

152. Who is the usual minister of Confirmation?

The bishop is the usual minister of Confirmation.

153. Why should all Catholics be confirmed?

All Catholics should be confirmed in order to be strengthened against the dangers to salvation and to be prepared better to defend their Catholic faith.

154. What is the Holy Eucharist?

The Holy Eucharist is a sacrament and a sacrifice. In the Holy Eucharist, under the appearances of bread and wine, the Lord Christ is contained, offered, and received.

155. When did Christ institute the Holy Eucharist?

Christ instituted the Holy Eucharist at the Last Supper, the night before He died.

Level 5 - Lesson 14

Catechism

156. **What happened at the Last Supper when Our Lord said: "This is My body … this is My blood"?**

    When Our Lord said, "This is My body," the bread was changed into His body; and when He said, "This is My blood," the wine was changed into His blood.

157. **Did anything of the bread and wine remain after they had been changed into Our Lord's body and blood?**

    After the bread and wine had been changed into Our Lord's body and blood, there remained only the appearances of bread and wine.

158. **What do we mean by the appearances of bread and wine?**

    By the appearances of bread and wine we mean their color, taste, weight, and shape.

159. **When did Christ give His priests the power to change bread and wine into His body and blood?**

    Christ gave His priests the power to change bread and wine into His body and blood when He said to the apostles at the Last Supper: "Do this in remembrance of Me."

160. **What is the Mass?**

    The Mass is the sacrifice of the New Law in which Christ, through the priest, offers Himself to God in an unbloody manner under the appearance of bread and wine.

161. **Is the Mass the same sacrifice as the sacrifice of the cross?**

    The Mass is the same sacrifice as the sacrifice of the cross.

162. **Is there any difference between the sacrifice of the cross and the Sacrifice of the Mass?**

    The manner in which the sacrifice is offered is different. On the cross Christ physically shed His blood and was physically slain, while in the Mass there is no physical shedding of blood nor physical death.

www.ingramcontent.com/pod-product-compliance
Lightning Source LLC
Chambersburg PA
CBHW040356010526
44108CB00049B/2924